SHIRT FRONT

a short and amazing history of Aussie Rules

"Like a good backman, Shirtfront is authoritative and doesn't back down from a contest. It captures the essence of 'our' great game by reminding us of all those who helped shape it."

Glenn Manton, former Carlton star

"Shirtfront weaves together the strands of history that make today's footy so rich, magical and engaging. This is THE footy book for younger readers, but this adult couldn't put it down."

Jeff Richardson, *"Coodabeen Champions"*

"Paula Hunt has the passion of a Ron Barassi address, the skill of James Hird, and a true supporter's love of Australian football. At last, footy literature that's not just for older readers."

David Allen, co-author of Fallen: The Ultimate Heroes

SHIRT FRONT

a short and amazing history of **Aussie Rules**

by Paula Hunt

First published in 2005 by
black dog books
15 Gertrude Street
Fitzroy Vic 3065
Australia
+61 3 9419 9406
+61 3 9419 1214 (fax)
dog@bdb.com.au
www.bdb.com.au

Designed by Blue Boat Design
Printed and bound in Australia by Griffin Press
Cover photograph of Jack Dyer: Dyer family.
Every effort has been made to trace and acknowledge copyright material. The author and publisher would be pleased to hear from any copyright holders who have not been acknowledged.

National Library of Australia
cataloguing-in-publication data:
Hunt, Paula, 1964- .
Shirtfront: a short and amazing history of Aussie Rules.

Bibliography.
Includes index.
ISBN 1 876372 66 4.

1. Australian football—History. I. Title.

796.336

10 9 8 7 6 5 4 3 2 1 5 6 7 8 / 0

To Peter, Venita, Shadae and Barb, for being there for all the spectacular victories and horrible losses.

Contents

Club List

Almost every club playing Australian football, whether it be in the AFL or in the local country league, has a nickname or two. Over the years those nicknames might have changed, and in some cases the nickname has become the club's official name (North Melbourne are now officially the Kangaroos and Footscray, the Western Bulldogs). Talk to a footy fan and these nicknames flow freely in conversation.

Adelaide	Crows
Brisbane	Bears, Lions
Carlton	Blues
Collingwood	Magpies, Pies
Essendon	Bombers, Dons
Fitzroy	Maroons, Lions
Footscray	Tricolours, Bulldogs
Fremantle	Dockers
Geelong	Pivotonians, Cats
Hawthorn	Maybllooms, Hawks
Melbourne	Redlegs, Fuchsias, Demons
North Melbourne	Shinboners, Kangaroos
Port Adelaide (AFL)	Power
Port Adelaide (SANFL)	Magpies
Richmond	Tigers
St Kilda	Saints
South Melbourne	Blood-stained Angels, Bloods, Swans
Sydney	Bloods, Swans
West Coast	Eagles

Abbreviations

AFL	Australian Football League
MCC	Melbourne Cricket Club
MCG	Melbourne Cricket Ground
NTFA	Northern Tasmanian Football Association
NWFA	North-Western Football Association (Tasmania)
SAFA	South Australian Football Association
SANFL	South Australian National Football League
SRFU	Southern Rugby Football Union
TFL	Tasmanian Football League
VFA	Victorian Football Association
VFL	Victorian Football League
WAFL	Western Australian Football League

Introduction

I love football. I have watched football while standing among the barrackers behind the goals at my local ground, from inside a corporate box while eating scones and jam, and from the stands at MCG on that last day in September. No matter where I am, I scream and holler for the players to "kick it down the guts" or to "man up". A victim of some self-held superstition, I refuse to wash my scarf during the season. By the last game of the home and away season it is flecked with bits of dried tomato sauce and reeks of long-ago devoured dims sims. I'm just your average footy fan.

What is it that draws us to Australian Rules football? No doubt it has something to do with the sheer physical spectacle that is each game. Screamers, long bombs and shirtfronts are all part of the attraction. But I have also enjoyed the bond with other fans. Those sitting in the MCC Members' Pavilion might look a bit different to the crowd that sits behind the floggers in the cheersquad, but the game is a great leveller and people are surprisingly similar when their team is winning (or losing). Right from the start, toffs and larrikins, sheilas and blokes, ladies and gentlemen all came out to watch the football.

When I started this book I thought I knew a fair bit about the history of the game, all the astonishing moments that have become part of footy folklore. But in the end I discovered I knew just a sliver of what had gone on

before. To understand just what makes those speckies so spectacular and those sheilas and blokes so passionate, you need to know the whole tale, from the beginning to now. So here it is!

The story of Australian Rules mirrors the society in which it was played. Sometimes that's a story of violence and bigotry. But more often, to idealists like me, football has made us a better community. The AFL's effort to break down racial barriers has been one of football's greatest achievements. It is hard now to imagine a game without indigenous players flying for the big marks or kicking goals from impossible angles.

Australian football is also a game that won't be budged. It provokes astonishing passion in the people who follow it, but it has been hard to export beyond the southern and western states of Australia. Despite all the attempts at expansion, the most important game of the season, the AFL grand final, is still played but a few hundred metres from where Scotch College and Melbourne Grammar played that first game nearly 150 years ago. For all that has changed, much more has stayed the same.

In his introduction to David Williamson's play about football politics, *The Club*, Ian Turner writes that Melbourne is, "an otherwise dour and inward-turning city, which has this one grand public passion." But he could be talking about Adelaide or Hobart or any of a hundred country towns. Places that are never quite so alive as when the Sherrin is in play.

The problem with trying to write a compact book about 150 years of history is not what is said, but what is left out. Many champions and many great games are not even mentioned in this book, and my account relies heavily on the Victorian competition. Not because the game outside of Victoria is any less fascinating, but because it simply became impossible to include it all.

Finally, a confession. I don't think you can write a book like this without admitting allegiances and mine lie with the Blues. One of the things about history is it doesn't always paint the ones you love in their best light. I have had to accept some home truths about the game and club I support. But in the end my passion for Australian Rules football is as strong as ever — after all, there is always next season.

Paula Hunt

Melbourne wasn't much more than a rustic town in 1851 when a cry of 'gold' echoed around the world. People flocked to the Victorian goldfields to make their fortunes but most ended up back in Melbourne when the gold ran dry. The city prospered — theatres and schools were built, and a hotel appeared on every corner. Cricket was popular, as were the horse races. Then a bloke called Tom Wills decided Melbourne needed a football club, but they would not play the football they played back 'home' in England. "We shall have a game of our own," he declared.

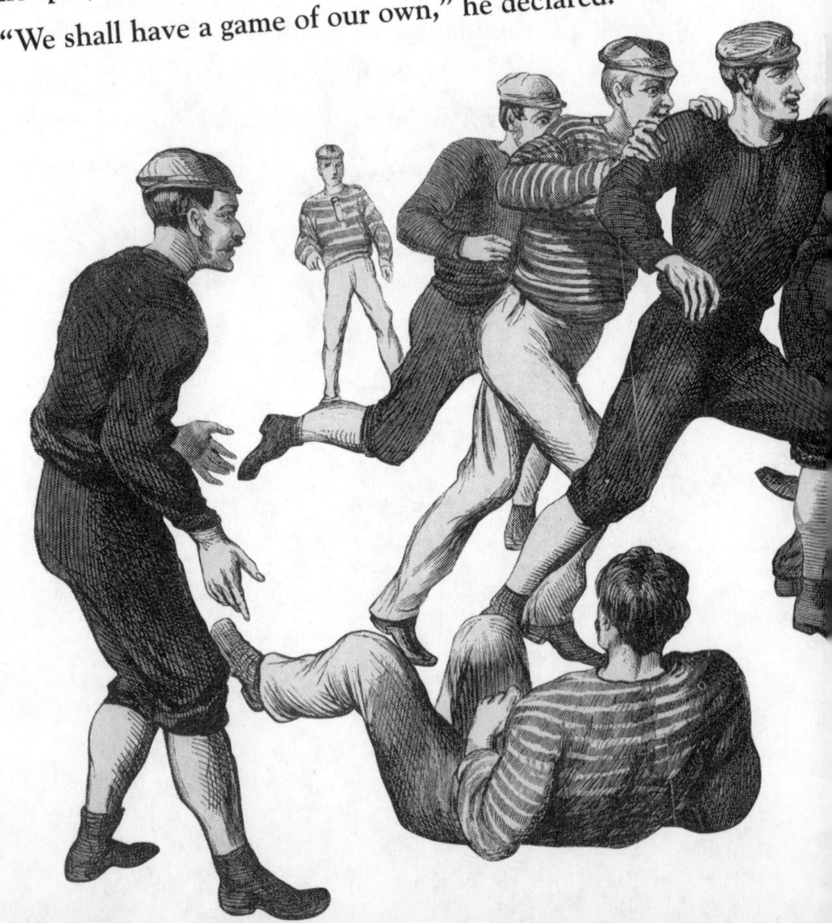

The First Bounce

1835 Tom Wills born.

1837 Governor Bourke declares Port Phillip a settlement.

1850 The colony of Victoria separates from New South Wales.

1851 Gold is discovered in Victoria.

1858 Tom Wills writes letter to *Bell's Life* suggesting the formation of a football club.

Melbourne Grammar plays Scotch College on Yarra Park.

Melbourne Football Club formed.

1859 Ten Rules of the Melbourne Football Club (the Melbourne Rules) written.

1860 Adelaide Football Club formed.

1861 Tom Wills's father and 18 others killed in Queensland.

1865 First Challenge Cup Series.

1877 Victorian Football Association (VFA) formed (included senior clubs Melbourne, Carlton, Hotham — later to be called North Melbourne — St Kilda and Albert Park).

South Australian Football Association formed.

1878 Geelong, Essendon and West Melbourne play as senior clubs in the VFA.

1879 South Melbourne play as a senior club in the VFA.

First interstate representatives match between Victoria and South Australia.

1880 Tom Wills commits suicide.

Beginning of the economic boom in Melbourne.

The 'first' game

On a winter's day in 1858, 80 boys, the sons of Melbourne's lawyers, doctors and bankers, gathered in the park next to the Melbourne Cricket Ground for a game of football.

Each team chose an umpire. Scotch chose their chemistry teacher John Macadam — his red hair and beard a sure sign of his Scottish heritage. Melbourne Grammar chose a man idolised in the new colony of Victoria as their champion cricketer, Tom Wills.

The goals were set up at either end of the park, so far from each other that over the scraggy uneven field those at one goal couldn't see those at the other. To move the ball along, the boys dodged gum trees, rocks, and a pack of 40 opposition players. A good high kick could have sent the ball up into the waiting limbs of those pesky gums where it would prop. The footballs, which had been imported from England, were made from specially treated pig or calf bladders that were hand-sewn in a casing of leather. Instead of calling for another ball, the players would stand below the tree waiting for the 'pigskin' to drop down, or if it was wedged in they'd send someone up to get it.

After several hours, Scotch scored a goal and the crowd of several hundred let out a cheer. But Melbourne Grammar wasn't prepared to go down without a fight. After some food and drink in the MCC Members' Pavilion to revive their spirits they returned to the field and managed an equaliser. When play had been going on for about five hours the light started to fade. The scores were level at a goal apiece (there was no such thing as a behind) so the teams agreed to meet again in two weeks' time. They did, but neither side managed a score. A third encounter two weeks after that was also scoreless. It was now the end of winter and time to start thinking about cricket. It could be said that this game took the entire season to play and ended in a draw.

"A grand football match will be played this day, between the Scotch College and the Church of England Grammar School, near the Melbourne Cricket Club ground. Luncheon at the pavilion. Forty a side. The game to commence at twelve o'clock."

Melbourne Morning Herald
7 August 1858

Smelbourne

By 1858, Melbourne had grown dramatically, from a little settlement in 1837 of 500 people, 100 000 sheep and a pub, to a small city with a university, gas-lit streets, several local newspapers, and a lot more than one pub. But there were still remnants of Melbourne's rugged start. Bushrangers still lurked in the scrub around the city. And because the city had expanded so quickly there had been little time to plan. Housing was a problem, but even more so was waste. The Yarra River was disgusting. Raw sewage and blood from the slaughter houses floated down the river into

Port Phillip Bay. In early Melbourne, every day the air was heavy with a poohey stench and death from disease was commonplace.

The Melbourne Cemetery had been moved to the site in Carlton in 1853, but it was badly designed. When it rained, the vaults and coffins would fill up and then the muck would ooze out and flow into Carlton and down the hill into the low-lying, working-class suburb of Collingwood. It was decades before the Magpies would be born but the rivalry between the two suburbs had its roots in the city's early history.

Gold had paved the way for Melbourne's growth. First discovered in the new colony in 1851, the lure of gold had seen thousands migrate to Victoria from around the world. But life on the goldfields was hard work, and the merchants made fortunes more often than the diggers. Defeated diggers returned to Melbourne and the city exploded. In a decade the population increased eight-fold.

Football was played on the goldfields. Scratch games played by mates. The rules were probably a hybrid of the games played back 'home' in England — games that would become rugby union and association football (soccer), with some local rules chucked in for good measure. Around Melbourne too, friends would get together for casual games of football.

The game between Scotch College and Melbourne Grammar wasn't really the first football game played in Melbourne, but it was important in the evolution of the game that became known as Aussie Rules—although if you'd seen the game that day you'd have been hard-pressed to recognise it.

From cocoons to butterflies

No individual can claim to be solely responsible for the inspiration that gave us Australian football, but Tom Wills comes close.

Tom Wills's grandfather was lucky to have escaped the hangman's noose when he was transported to Australia for highway robbery. But despite the stigma of his convict father's past, Tom's father made good in the new country, becoming a printer and publisher and then a rich sheep owner. Tom was born in 1835 and when he was not much more than an infant he went droving sheep with his parents, camping out each night under the stars. He played with the local Aboriginal children and even learned their language, singing songs they'd taught him.

When he was just 14, he was sent on a rugged sea journey halfway around the world to go to Rugby School in England. The trip took months and the ship had to navigate the treacherous Cape Horn. The school was obviously unaware of Tom's grandfather. If they'd known Tom was the descendant of a convict, they might well have been appalled. At Rugby School, Tom played cricket and football (rugby style), developing a real talent for sport.

He was a bit of a sensation when he arrived back in Victoria a confident 21-year-old. He was a talented

cricketer and quickly became the Melbourne Cricket Club's champion. He was a flashy dresser, wore his hair fashionably long and must have been a bit of a hit with the ladies. Melbourne was still a town linked very strongly to the values of England. In polite society there were protocols to be observed. But in this atmosphere of stiff propriety, around town Tom Wills became simply known as Tommy. If you mentioned Tommy, everyone knew who you were talking about.

Cricket had as much to do with the development of the new football code as any football played in England. Tom loved cricket and so did his fellow Victorians — they were cricket mad. They also had developed a deep rivalry with New South Wales and there was nothing they wanted more than to beat NSW at cricket.

"Sir — Now that cricket has been put aside for some months to come, and cricketers have assumed somewhat of the chrysalis nature (for a time only 'tis sure), but at length will burst forth in all their varied hues, rather than allow this state of torpor to creep over them, and stifle their now supple limbs, why can they not, I say, form a foot-ball club, and form a committee of three or more to draw up a code of laws?"

Tom Wills in *Bell's Life,* an early sports magazine.

A month before the Melbourne Grammar /Scotch College game Tom published a now-famous letter in the local sports newspaper. He suggested forming a football or rifle club to help keep the cricketers fit over winter and increase their chances of beating New South Wales. Luckily football won the day and late in the winter of 1858 the Melbourne Football Club was formed.

The Melbourne Football Club is one of the oldest football clubs of any code in the world, probably the oldest club of any code to be playing at senior level, and is still going strong today.

Marks and free kicks

After the 1858–1859 cricket season, Wills and his mates JB Thompson, Tom Smith and William Hammersley sat down to write the 10 'Melbourne Rules' for football. These are the oldest set of written rules for any form of football that exists today, older than American football, the modern version of Gaelic football, rugby and soccer. It is amazing that in a society that emulated everything British, these men decided not to play the football they had learnt in the 'home' country, but to develop a game of their own. It was based in part on the English game, but made for the local conditions.

Of those first 10 rules, two are really interesting when we think of the differences between Australian Rules and other football codes today.

- A player who catches the ball directly from a kick can call 'mark' and then have a free kick from the marked position. (Players would mark the ground where they

took their mark, sometimes with a hat or by gouging the grass with their boot.)

- In no circumstances can the ball be thrown when in play.

The rules didn't say what shape or size the ground or ball must be. Historian Geoffrey Blainey believes that the early footballs were round, and that the grounds were rectangular, not oval.

The rules for what we call soccer were written up a couple of years later, and in 1864 someone writing under the pen-name 'Free Kick' wrote an article suggesting the English Football Association had somehow seen a copy of the Melbourne Rules and had used them as the basis for the first rules of soccer. Soccer had been played in streets of working-class Britain for years, but no one had bothered to write down the rules.

In 1980 Bill Gray, curator of the MCC museum, found the handwritten copy of the first set of Melbourne Rules in a tin in the bowels of the MCG.

Possum skins

The Djab wurrung and Jardwadjali Aboriginal clans living in western Victoria called their game marn-grook — 'game ball'. They originally made their footballs out of possum skin filled with charcoal. Later a lighter football was made using a strong twine of possum hair. The object of the game was to kick the ball as high as you could and the other players would attempt to catch it. Players would leap, soaring up to 1.5 metres into the air to catch the ball. The game could go on for hours and it appears there was no scoring; it was played for pure enjoyment.

For years people have wondered whether Tom Wills, who grew up among the Aborigines of the Western Districts, knew of marn-grook and whether it influenced Australian football. The similarity between leaping for catches in marn-grook and high marking in Australian Rules seems strong. And while high marking doesn't directly affect the score, it is without doubt the most spectacular part of the game we love.

Some historians do not believe there is much proof of a connection between the two games. High marking wasn't a feature of Australian football until the mid 1870s and some would say it wasn't perfected until the 1880s when Charles 'Commotion' Pearson from Essendon started to leap for the ball. Still, research goes on to see if more evidence can be found that links Australia's indigenous game with its indigenous people.

Colden

By the end of 1858, there were at least three informal clubs: Melbourne, South Yarra and St Kilda (not the same St Kilda football club of today). A year later Tom Wills

was involved in the formation of the Geelong Football Club. In the early days most players were white-collar workers or students. Most manual labourers worked Saturdays and didn't have time to play football. But things were changing — a few years before, the stonemasons in Melbourne had become the first workers in the world to win an eight-hour working day.

Henry Colden Antill Harrison, known as Colly or Colden to his mates, was Tom Wills's cousin and his brother-in-law. He would go on to become one of the game's first footy superstars.

Like his cousin, Colden spent his childhood on his father's sheep station, but his dad wasn't as successful as Tom's and in the end the family gave it away and moved to Melbourne. Colden's father then caught a bad case of gold fever, and he and his son headed up to the goldfields. But Colden, still only 14, didn't take to life on the goldfields — rotten food and flea-infested bedding was not for him. He came back to Melbourne and started a career as a public servant. Colden's father remained on the goldfields where he was one of the agitators against the high taxes on diggers.

Colden was around 179 cm tall (5 foot 10 inches) and 80 kg (12 stone 8 pounds) — the height and weight of a modern-day midfielder. Where his cousin was a natural cricketer, Colden was a natural runner and a natural footballer. Colden missed the first season of football and was not there when Tom and the others wrote the first rules, but after that he became one of the most influential players of the time. It was Colden who changed the style of the game when he started running with the ball. The game became faster and more exciting to watch. To stop Colden's run, a rule was added requiring a player to bounce the ball intermittently while running with it.

Colden, despite being a public servant, liked football to be tough, or in his words "manly". In 1864, Carlton Football Club was formed. By that time many working-class men had Saturday afternoon off and could play football. Victoria was at the forefront of workers' rights and this was important in the development of the game. It meant everyone could come to watch or play, not just those of the privileged classes. Carlton became one of the first clubs to play working-class men. They played a far more aggressive game and that suited Colden. Once, when he had to defend his rough tactics, he said, "football is essentially a rough game all the world over, and it is not suitable for men-poodles or milksops."

Over his football career Colden captained Melbourne, Richmond and Geelong, and was named Champion of the Colony in 1862, 1863, 1866, 1867 and 1869. He was simply a football superstar. He went on to become an administrator and by the mid 1870s he was known around town as 'the father of football'.

Barrackers

Right from the start people turned out in droves to watch football, catching public transport (horse-drawn carriages)

or just walking to the ground to cheer on the players. And they weren't just there for a day out, they took football seriously. Sometimes, fans in their tailored jackets and boxer hats would venture out into the middle of the playing field so they could get a better view of the game. Even women, in their long frilly frocks, were known to wander into the line of fire for a closer look. Many found themselves knocked over unceremoniously when they got just a little too close to the action.

While Australian football was drawing crowds of up to 10 000, the 1872 FA Cup in England was watched by only 2000 fans.

By the end of the 1860s, five to ten thousand would regularly turn up to cheer on their team and boo the opposition. Melbournians are renowned for turning up in great numbers for all sorts of sporting events, but their passion for football is unsurpassed.

These days the word 'barracker' is used all over the world to describe enthusiastic and vocal fans but it originated in Melbourne in the early days of Australian football. Some people believe the word barracker comes from the Irish word *barrack* which meant to brag, while others believe it's derived from the Aboriginal word *borak* which means to ridicule. But there is one other interesting possibility. In the 1860s the soldiers stationed at the barracks in St Kilda Road were free to play football on Saturday afternoons and they became keen players and vocal supporters. Some people believe we can thank those soldiers for the term 'barracker'.

People lived where they worked and followed the football team in their suburb. Over the years rivalries between the various clubs were born, adding excitement, as well as passion, to the games.

"Ex-Cabinet Ministers and their families, members of Parliament, professional and tradesmen, free selectors and squatters, clerks, shopmen, bagmen, mechanics, larrikins, betting men, publicans, barmaids (very strongly represented), working-girls and half the world."

Description in the *Argus* newspaper of the crowd at a Carlton/Melbourne match in 1876.

Melbourne Football Club saw themselves as the sacred keepers of the game and Carlton decided they should knock high and mighty Melbourne off their pedestal. It was the first great rivalry and fans would flock to see the clashes between the two teams. Carlton fans were passionate and they didn't hide it. It wasn't unknown for mad Carlton supporters to run onto the field and try and attack the opposition players. At one match the

huge crowd spilled onto the field. The Melbourne players were forced to group together and charged the Carlton mob, like they were unruly cattle, to disperse them. These rivalries added to the spectacle of football, even if they did sometimes get out of hand.

For the first two decades there was no admission fee and anyone was welcome to come and watch. Arguably more than any other football code, Aussie Rules has traditionally included everyone: gentlemen and ladies, blokes and sheilas. When an admission fee was finally charged, it was small and most people could afford it.

Victorian Rules

Victorians all over the state were as mad about football as the fans in Melbourne. When Hamilton sent its team to Warrnambool, the main businesses at the port closed their doors on the afternoon of the match.

Ballarat fielded a senior football club in 1862. Much of the team was made up of miners, who had shorter hours than many manual workers. These were not men who spent their days behind a desk pushing a pen; these men had broad shoulders and calluses on their hands, and the game they played was rugged. By 1870 railways had reached Echuca, Colac, Ballarat, Bendigo and Geelong, allowing teams to travel to play one another.

In 1865, the Melbourne Athletic Sports Committee presented a "handsome" trophy, the Challenge Cup, for competition. This was the year that football in Melbourne started to get organised. Clubs would 'challenge' each other to matches and the cup would get handed to the winner. Over the year it changed hands many times. At the end of the season, newspaper reporters would vote to declare 'champion team' of the year. Although it is hard to believe that the reporters could be taken seriously after this account of a goal: "...a splendid drop kick with a great deal of screw on, sending the ball six or seven times round a tree in immediate vicinity before it went flying through the centre of the posts and won the game."

Australian football was still a low-scoring affair in those days, a few goals a game. In 1866 South Yarra played 14 games; eight ended in draws.

Over the next decade, football continued to grow in popularity and become more structured. In 1872 Melbourne became the first club with a real football look, blue guernsey and knickerbockers, red socks (which gave them the nickname Redlegs) and red cap. The bigger clubs were starting to establish large followings. In 1877 the Victorian Football Association (VFA) was formed to deal with the rules, general management and promotion of the game, and the Challenge Cup was replaced by the VFA premiership.

Territories won

Football made its way to Adelaide very early on. The Adelaide Football Club was formed in 1860. The club would split into two (pink caps and blue caps) on match

days and effectively play against itself. Football in Adelaide was different to that played in Melbourne. No doubt there were some different rules, but it also held a different place in the social life of the city. All sorts of dignitaries, dressed in their finest gear, would come out to watch the football in Adelaide. When there were breaks in play, a band hired for the occasion would pump out a tune. The next day in the newspaper the match report would list all the politicians, church ministers and businessmen in the crowd, but forget to tell the readers the score.

But by the late 1870s football had begun to imbed itself into Adelaide culture much as it had done in Melbourne, ensuring for all-time South Australia would be part of footy's heartland. The South Australians formed their own association the same year as the Victorians, and drew up their own rules. In 1879 the two colonies played each other in a state representative match. The South Australians developed a rivalry with the Victorians. But unlike the Victorians and New South Welshmen who fought their battles out on the cricket pitch, the South Australians and Victorians preferred the footy field.

The early days of football in Tasmania are a little cloudy. We are not exactly sure when footy was first played there, or what rules they used. Still, we know that by the mid 1860s there were games of football being played at various places across the island. Perhaps in the end it was the close proximity between Tasmania and Melbourne that ensured the game would settle there. The Tasmanians too, developed a great rivalry—the island split in two, north and south. For years several competitions were played on the apple isle.

When the men of the barracks arrived at the town of Perth in 1868 for a tour of duty, they brought with them their wives, their children and a new game, Australian football. They played several games in the year they were stationed there, but when they left it looked like Perth might have experienced its one and only season of Aussie Rules football. It was 15 years before footy re-emerged out west. For a while the town was caught in a tussle between rugby and Australian football, but, in the end, Aussie Rules became the football game of choice and by the late 1880s Perth had four teams and an Australian football association of its own.

Territories lost

Why didn't Aussie Rules catch on in Sydney and Brisbane?

Australian football was played in Sydney and Brisbane in the mid 1860s but the Southern Rugby Football Union (SRFU) made sure the new code never took off. The SRFU banned their players from playing Australian football and they controlled the grounds so they also made sure there was nowhere to play it.

In 1877 the Waratahs defied the SRFU's edict and played Carlton in two matches, one of rugby, one of Victorian Rules. Not surprisingly each team won the match played

to the rules of their code. The games attracted some of the biggest football crowds recorded in Sydney at the time and there was a lively debate in the press on the merits of each code.

Perhaps the real reason the new code of football didn't take off was because of the great rivalry between the two colonies of Victoria and New South Wales. This was best described in an article in the *Melbourne Punch* newspaper in 1889, "The great objection to the rules in NSW was that they were styled 'The Victorian Rules of Football'. Had they been dubbed the Scandinavian rules, well and good; but Victorian—perish the thought."

It also has to be remembered that for this short period of time, Victoria was a larger, more prosperous colony than its older northern relative. There was a growing move for nationalisation coming from Victoria. This push was not received as enthusiastically in NSW. Rugby was an English game, and those in power did everything they could to ensure that the game played back 'home' remained the game played in NSW.

Goodbye Tommy

When he was 26, Tom Wills swapped life in the growing metropolis of Melbourne, with its gas-lit streets and horrendous smells, for starlit nights and the aroma of eucalyptus in the Queensland bush. There he helped drove thousands of sheep to his father's new property.

Tom was away getting supplies when Aborigines attacked the camp killing 19 people including his father. It was the biggest slaughter of whites by blacks in Australia's history. In the retributions that followed, probably three times as many Aborigines were killed. There is much debate about what set the attack off—many years later Tom's brother, Cedric, wrote that Tom had never accepted the whites' version of events and thought it was caused by a white settler shooting two Aborigines for the theft of some sheep that were later found wandering around. Despite what he told Cedric later, at the time Tom remained at the station, managing its affairs, and apparently vowed to shoot any Aborigines who came onto his land. After a while he gave away the life of a station owner and returned to his sporting career in Melbourne.

Back in Melbourne he continued to play football. Over his career he played for and captained Melbourne, Richmond and Geelong. He played cricket with Victoria, MCC, Richmond and Geelong. He also started drinking excessively.

Tom's relationship with black Australia was a complex one. A few years after the events in Queensland, he coached the Aboriginal Cricket Team. In a society of extreme racism, Tom could count black Australians as playmates in childhood and team-mates in adulthood. But he also had to contend with his own demons about what happened in Queensland, both to his father and to the Aborigines killed in retribution.

The Aboriginal Cricket Team played the Melbourne Cricket Club on the MCG on Boxing Day, where they were soundly beaten, before going on to tour England in 1868. Tom did not travel with them to England, but the tour was a rousing success. They won 14 games, lost 14 and drew 18.

Despite his drinking, Tom maintained his skill with bat and ball. He continued to play football until the ripe old age of 41. When he left his playing days behind he stayed in the administration of football—he was keen to export the game around the world. But he had also begun to suffer bouts of crippling depression.

1880 was a controversial year for Melbourne. Tom Wills committed suicide in May. In November, Judge Redmond Barry sentenced Ned Kelly to be hanged. "I will see you where I go," Ned told the judge. Barry died 12 days later. Redmond Barry had been the inaugural president of the Carlton Cricket Club and was involved in the formation of the Carlton Football Club in 1864.

Finally he was in such a bad state he was put under the constant care of a male attendant. He was at home in Heidelberg, alone with his wife one morning—his attendant apparently having left him alone for a while—when he picked up a pair of scissors. His wife understood what her husband was about to do, but she was not strong enough to stop him. Tom plunged the heavy steel blades of the scissors into his chest three times, taking his life.

After his death, Tom Wills's name was shunned and his extraordinary contribution to Australian football was forgotten. In recent times the Melbourne Cricket Club restored Tom Wills's grave. His gravestone reads, "Founder of Australian Football and Champion Cricketer of his time."

Australian Rules

The rules of Australian football have never been carved in stone. Most of the various colonies wrote their own rules and the different controlling bodies could not agree. Even today it is unusual to go through a season without a rule change. The following list is far from complete but it notes a few of the more interesting facts about the rules.

Offside

One of the distinctive features of Australian Rules is the lack of an offside rule, which exists in both rugby and soccer. The absence of this rule was seen as the biggest chasm between rugby and Australian Rules in the early years.

Free

A year after the first 'Melbourne Rules' were written, a rule was added that allowed the captains (there were no field umpires) to award a free kick when an infringement had been made.

Ball!

A rule preventing a player holding onto the ball when tackled by an opponent was added in 1874.

High tackle

Rabbiting (tackling a player from below the hips) was outlawed in 1874. By 1887 you could not grab a player around the neck and sling him to the ground.

Little mark

In the early days the rules did not specify the distance a kick must travel to be awarded a mark. In the 1870s players realised they could work the ball around (say if on an impossible angle for a shot for goal) using short kicks which resulted in 'little marks'. Sometimes players would throw the ball rather than kick it, which was illegal.

On the full

Until 1969 a ball kicked out on the full was thrown in by the umpire.

Two flags

Flags were being used to indicate the scoring of goals or behinds in Tasmania in 1884.

High marks

In the 1904 Grand Final, a Carlton forward took a screamer over a Fitzroy defender, in the process putting his knees into his opponent's back. The umpire awarded a free against him, which was correct but controversial. Fans wanted to see the high marks. The rules were changed to allow for unintentional interference.

Goals and behinds

In the beginning only the goals were counted, there was no such thing as a behind. There were two kick off posts from which the defending team could kick-in a ball that had been kicked out of bounds along the forward line. Unofficially teams would keep a note of these 'near misses'. When the VFL was formed, it started a scoring system of six points for a goal and one point for a behind.

Number of players

In 1899 the VFL reduced teams from 20 per side to 18. The VFA changed the number of players per side several times, to anywhere between 16 and 18. The VFL stuck with 18.

Interchange

The interchange bench was first used in 1978. Until then teams had a reserves but once the reserve took to the field, the man he replaced could not re-enter the game.

Centre ruck

In 1980 a line was drawn across the centre circle and the rule changed to prevent the two ruckmen wrestling. This controversial rule came about after one game where Peter Moore and Gary Dempsey had wrestled at each centre bounce.

Reported

Up until 1908 only the field umpire could report a player, after that time the boundary umpires were also given the power to report players. Two years later this responsibility was extended to their colleagues behind the goals.

If you don't mind umpire

In 1976 it was decided that the days when one field umpire could manage the game alone were well and truly over, and the number of field umpires was increased from one to two. Seventeen years later another field umpire was added, bringing the total to three. According to the fans, no matter how many umpires litter the field, they still can't get it right.

How long?

In 1981 the distance a player could travel with the ball before the ball had to make contact with the ground (bounced or touched to the ground) was increased from 10 metres to 15. In 2002 the distance a kick had to travel before a player could claim a mark was also increased from 10 metres to 15.

Bootmakers, Stockbrokers and Larrikins

J. Smith

T. Beecham

During the 1880s, the population of Melbourne almost doubled. It was the biggest city in Australia and there was plenty of work for everyone. Marvellous Melbourne they called it. And it was a boon for football too. The popularity of the game soared, crowds grew and allegiances were forged. But with every up there is a down. Early in the next decade, depression hit with full force, and an unpleasant side to the footy barracker was revealed.

C. ROWLANDS

M. DONAGHY

1883 John Mills (Ballarat Imperials) is believed to be the first player to die from injuries sustained on the footy field.

1885 Football association formed in Western Australia.

1890 The depression hits.

1893 Banks close their doors without warning.

1896 Collingwood and South Melbourne play off at the end of the year to determine the premiers — this was the first unrecognised grand final.

1897 Several clubs (Collingwood, Essendon, Fitzroy, Melbourne, South Melbourne, Geelong, St Kilda and Carlton) break away to form the Victorian Football League (VFL).

Essendon are the first VFL premiers.

1898 Fitzroy wins the first VFL grand final.

1902 First time a VFL grand final is played at the MCG.

Marvellous Melbourne

In the 1880s a working man would knock off at one or two o'clock on a Saturday afternoon, rush home to one of the working-class suburbs like North Melbourne or Fitzroy, and scrub up before heading out to the football. If his team was playing at home he'd walk to the ground, having to dodge the open sewers that ran down every street. He was used to Melbourne's pongy aroma. If his team was playing away, he might get there by cable tram or suburban steam train. When he arrived, he'd pay his sixpence (5 cents) and gather with the rest of the large crowd around the boundary. Thanks to the economic boom everyone from "Collingwood bootmakers to St Kilda stockbrokers" could afford the sixpence to see a match.

If he was at Albert Park to watch South Melbourne play, bookmakers would walk around yelling out their odds. At the MCG gambling was banned so the bookmakers had to be discreet. At the ground he would rub shoulders with everyone from politicians to cab drivers. Refined ladies would parade by in their bright clothing, parasols under their arms while the barmaids wore their club colours pinned to their hats.

On the ground, the game was higher scoring, faster and players had started to leap into the air to take impossible marks. Sleeveless guernseys had become popular and the ladies were treated to the spectacle of scantily clad, muscular men pursuing the football.

The crowd was glued to the action. Richard Twopeny

noted in his collection of essays of the time, *Town Life in Australia*, of the 10 000 people at a match, nearly all were intensely interested in the game. "A good football match in Melbourne is one of the sights of the world," he declared.

After the game there was no shortage of public houses where a footy fan could drop in for a 'nobbler' (drink) with his mates.

Dying to play

In 1883 John Mills, Captain of the Ballarat Imperials, was kicked by another player. He went home but died later from a ruptured intestine. He was probably the first player to die from an incident on the field.

Despite the physical nature of the game, fatalities have been rare. Although some Carlton faithful might argue that the death of one of the game's greatest players of the era, George Coulthard, was also a consequence of what happened on the footy field.

Carlton champion George Coulthard, and Hotham's Joey Tankard, never liked each other. When Carlton recruited Tankard at the beginning of 1882 he was only at the club a short time before he and Coulthard were brawling. Tankard headed back to Hotham (North Melbourne) before he'd played even one game for the Blues.

Tankard's first game back at Hotham was against Carlton, and his opponent was Coulthard. It didn't take long before the two were exchanging blows. Both players were reported by the umpire and suspended for the rest of the year.

This upset Coulthard and Carlton. Coulthard, they argued, had only hit back after Tankard threw the first punch. The VFA didn't budge. Carlton said they wouldn't play again until the suspension was lifted. And sure enough at their next match, against Melbourne, they walked onto the ground but left without kicking a ball when Coulthard was refused permission to play. It was a football strike.

Eventually Carlton backed down and began playing again. Tankard's suspension was lifted after five matches but Coulthard's stood. Coulthard, the man who had been the VFA's leading goal kicker in 1879 and Carlton's greatest player of the era, never played again.

A year after he'd retired Coulthard became sick with tuberculosis and died. He was just 27 years old. Coulthard had been a hero to the people of Carlton, and when he died the entire suburb went into mourning. And there were plenty who thought his death had more to do with his treatment by the game's authorities than the tuberculosis in his lungs.

Larrikins, hooligans and roughs

By the late 1880s violence in the crowd was becoming a real problem. Groups of young men and women, dressed in frock coats, top hats and their club colours, harassed the opposition team and beat up their supporters. They were known as larrikins.

It was so bad at Richmond that the club nearly folded. Fans were too frightened to go and watch Richmond play so they would walk to the nearby East Melbourne ground to watch Essendon instead. At Carlton, roughs would throw stones at the opposition team.

In 1886 one train trip from Geelong nearly ended in tragedy when team rivalries got completely out of hand. Two thousand Geelong supporters chartered a couple of trains to take them to Melbourne to watch their team play South Melbourne. Neither team had been defeated for the year, and this game was likely to decide the premiers. Outside Newport someone dislodged sections of the track in an attempt to crash the trains. Luckily it was discovered in time.

Just as crowd behaviour was hitting rock bottom, so did Australia's economy. The boom was over. Depression hit in early 1893 when the banks closed their doors without warning. Factories closed down and soup kitchens were set up to feed the poor. Housing became so cheap that rent for a week was about the same as the cost for a family to go to the football (two shillings or 20 cents).

But football survived. For a lot of people football was not a luxury, but a necessity. Collingwood was an inner-city industrial suburb and its supporters would have been among the worst hit by the depression, yet when Collingwood Football Club was formed in 1892 they signed up 400 new members. And Footscray, another working-class suburb, still managed to get crowds of 7000 to their games.

But generally attendances to football games dropped. Players were affected too. Most were working men. If there was no work in Melbourne they hit the road. Some of the greatest players headed to the country or out west in search of work.

White maggots

At the very first games, each team nominated someone to act as a goal umpire, but disputes during play were handled by the captains. The first central umpire officiated at a Carlton/Melbourne match in 1866. Like the players he was not paid. But by 1883 large amounts of money were being bet on the results of each game. The VFA was worried that an umpire might be bribed. They decided to nominate their own umpire (although surprisingly the goal umpires were still selected by the teams) and pay him £1 ($2) a week. The umpires paid dearly for that pound.

Up until then, the crowds and newspapers treated the umpire with some respect. He was, after all, giving up his own time to umpire the game. But once he was paid he was seen as a professional and open to criticism. It was the start of a rocky relationship between the umpire and the fans.

One of football's most infamous incidents occurred in 1896 in a game between North Melbourne and Collingwood. Umpire Roberts was tough on North Melbourne's use of the 'little mark'. At that time there was no distance a kick had to travel before a player could claim a mark. That

meant crafty players could throw the ball to their team-mates who would then cry "mark". Roberts, a retired Carlton player, obviously thought this was North's tactic and consistently awarded free kicks against them. North Melbourne was a working-class suburb and its fans, later dubbed the Shinboners because the local butchers would hang club colours in their windows, were aggressively loyal. They became murderous over what they saw as unfair umpiring.

At the end of the game as Roberts tried to get to the pavilion, the North supporters ran onto the ground and attacked him, knocking him to the ground. To the shock of Melbourne society, some of the attackers were women brandishing umbrellas and hatpins, and screaming out "job 'im with yer umbreller" and "kill the little beast". Luckily for Roberts, two players, North Melbourne's McDougall and Collingwood's Bill Proudfoot, came to his

"The woman barracker, indeed, has become one of the most objectionable of football surroundings. On some grounds they actually spit in the faces of players as they come to the dressing-rooms, or wreak their spite much more maliciously with long hat pins," wrote the *Argus* newspaper after umpire Roberts was attacked after the 1896 game between North Melbourne and Collingwood.

aid. Proudfoot was a big ruckman and a police constable, but even he was overcome by the ferocity of the crowd. When they finally made it back to the pavilion, all three men collapsed. The newspapers had a field day calling it "the greatest disgrace of all time in Australian football."

Some players too, showed little respect for umpires. Collingwood's Dick Condon was a brilliant footballer, but he was also a brawler. He fought with everyone: team-mates, officials, as well as the opposition. Still, in 1899 he replaced Bill Proudfoot, umpire Robert's saviour, as captain of the Magpies. His stint as captain didn't last. The next year, he was playing in a game against Melbourne when umpire 'Ivo' Crapp awarded a free kick against him. Condon was livid. His short fuse was lit, and he made a comment about the umpire's girlfriend that was way out of line. Umpire Crapp reported him and he was suspended for life. The penalty seemed extremely harsh but Collingwood didn't help Condon with his

Bill Proudfoot—one of the players who saved umpire Roberts when he was attacked by the North Melbourne supporters—played in Collingwood's 1903 Grand Final team under an assumed name, Wilson, because the police commissioner had banned policemen from playing football.

appeal, perhaps relieved to be rid of him. Eighteen months after his suspension Condon's third appeal was successful and he returned to football. But Condon's temper hadn't been quelled. His return to Collingwood ended several years later when he was suspended for causing dissension. He spent a year as an umpire in Tasmania before a stint coaching and playing for Richmond. He left Richmond less than two years later after he once again upset team-mates. Dick Condon is the only Collingwood 10-year player not to be made a life member of the club.

The umpires were not just punching bags for the fans and the players — clubs also had their bone to pick with the men in white. Port Adelaide, playing the South Australian competition in 1902, told the game's administrators that they would forfeit their semifinal against South Adelaide rather than play under the direction of umpire Phil Kneebone. The SAFA didn't like Port Adelaide's attitude and promptly disqualified them.

The split

Football was supposed to be an amateur sport where players played for the love of the game, but in reality many were given good jobs by wealthy supporters or money for expenses. To stop this, the VFA decided they would manage the money, giving each club a small amount for administration, the rest to go to charity. The wealthier clubs were horrified.

On the eve of the final game for 1896, Geelong,

Essendon, South Melbourne, Fitzroy, Collingwood and Melbourne met to finalise plans to break away and form the Victorian Football League. They decided to invite two other clubs, Carlton and St Kilda, to join. Carlton, who had been one of the strongest clubs in the first three decades of competition, had fallen on hard times and were lucky to be asked.

In 1897, the VFL took to the ground. The VFA continued to run its competition. For the next century the greatest battle in Victorian football was not between two rival clubs, but between two rival administrations, the VFA and the VFL.

The VFL went about making some rule changes, but perhaps their most important innovation was the grand final. In the Challenge Cup, the news reporters would assess the year's results and then declare the Champion Team of the Year. Not surprisingly this caused lots of arguments. In 1888, the VFA introduced a system of points (four for a win, two for a draw and none for a loss). The premier was the club with the greatest number of points at the end of the year. If two teams had the same number of points, the team that kicked the most goals for the year won.

In 1896, South Melbourne and Collingwood finished the season on equal points and equal goals for and against. There was no way to separate them except to play a grand final. This first, unrecognised, grand final was played in the first week of October. It was also the last time these two teams, and six others, would play in the VFA.

When the VFL commenced its competition the next year they decided to have the top four teams at the end of the season play off in a round robin competition to determine a premier. By the following year they had a complicated system that lead to a single game at the end of the season. The grand final was born.

The grand final was unique to Australian Rules football. It ensured the excitement of the season carried through from the very first to the last game. There were no sure things. A team could dominate the competition but in the end it came down to that last single game of the year.

As every footy fan knows there is nothing quite like the knot in your stomach when you are sitting at the MCG on that last Saturday in September, your team is warming up on the sacred turf and you are waiting for the ball to be bounced. Two hours later you are either in seventh heaven or crying into your scarf. A grand final is an emotional affair whether it is for the senior national competition, a state trophy or a country league.

There are a million grand final stories, not all of them grand. Imagine being a Tiger's fan in 1904. Richmond had made the grand final but, as Port Adelaide had two years before, they told the VFA that they would forfeit the game if umpire Allen officiated. The VFA didn't like being told what to do and nominated Allen as the umpire. True to their word, Richmond forfeited, breaking every black and gold heart. North Melbourne won the VFA grand final without scoring a goal.

The fans only had themselves to blame a year later when Mersey took on Devonport in the NWFA grand final in Tasmania. Mersey was well ahead when the crowd invaded the ground. Despite all the efforts of the players and officials they couldn't be shifted so the game was declared "finished for the day". It was arranged that the two teams would meet up again in four weeks' time to determine a winner. A month later Mersey turned up to play but there was no Devonport. Mersey went out onto the field, kicked eight goals and was declared the premiers.

107 yards

Albert Thurgood, 'Albert the Great' to his fans, was arguably the best player of his time. He was a champion in a champion team, Essendon. He was tall, well-built, and a fabulous kick. In 1899, one of his place kicks, kicked in practice, was recorded as a whopping 98.5 meters (107 yards 2 feet 1 inch), the longest kick ever recorded in Australian football. Thurgood was an amazing athlete and it was said he could run 92 metres (100 yards) in just over 10 seconds. He could play almost any position on the field, moving from the ruck to the forward-line or the back-line as his team required. He first played for Essendon between 1892 and 1894, helping them to successive premierships. In 1893 and 1894 he kicked 63 goals in the season, a record that held for 21 years.

In one sensational game that year, he single-handedly saved the day. Essendon were down to Melbourne by three

goals with only four minutes to go. In those days a team would be happy if they scored five goals a game, so the fans must have thought that the game was all over. That was until Albert the Great was moved onto the ball. He dominated the last minutes of play and scored four goals to win the game. And one of his goals came from an 82-metre (90 yard) kick.

But when Thurgood was in his early twenties, Melbourne was in the grip of the depression so he headed off to Fremantle for work. As popular as football was, it wasn't a professional sport and players had to think of themselves and their families first. Essendon supporters must have been devastated. Over in the west, Thurgood played for Fremantle, helping them to the premiership, while back home Essendon slumped without their star. He was not only a great player, but also had the ability to inspire the rest of the team.

After a few years Thurgood came back to Melbourne and his old club, Essendon. He hadn't lost any of his skill. In 1901, he was the best player on the ground, kicking long bombs and pulling down soaring marks, when Essendon knocked off the Magpies in the grand final.

The end of Thurgood's career was not as glorious as the start. In 1902, he became the first Essendon player in the VFL to be suspended for striking, and after an unusually poor performance in the grand final he was accused of playing 'dead'. In fact Collingwood had been tagging the champion, and at half-time had swapped the tagger for a fresher player. This was an unusual tactic at the time and reduced 'Albert the Great' to 'Albert the Mortal'. An inquiry into the accusations of bribery cleared Thurgood, but his relationship with Essendon never really recovered, and he announced his retirement. He played a few games for Essendon in 1906 but an injury ruined his comeback.

Rabbit-proof fence

In 1905 Bert Franks was playing for North Fremantle when he had to give the footy away and go bush for work. He was in the outback repairing rabbit-proof fences when he got a letter from his football club telling him they'd found him a job in Perth and to come back straightaway so he could play next week. The only problem was that Bert was miles from anywhere and he didn't have a car. So he packed up his belongings and started walking to the nearest railway station, 180 kilometres away. He didn't have much food on him but the few farmhouses he passed along the way gave him handouts that kept him going. After four days of walking under the Western Australian sun, he made it to the station and boarded the train. He played the next day and was one of the best on ground.

Gentle Annies

By 1907 football attendances were back up. The economy was recovering and the larrikin element had been somewhat controlled.

Women have always been enthusiastic football

supporters, accounting for more than 40 per cent of the crowd at most footy matches. Why Australian football manages to interest so many women remains a great talking point. It is hard to think of another sport where women don't compete at the elite level, but where there is such a high percentage of female supporters. Some people think the speed and open play make it an interesting spectacle for women. But perhaps just as importantly it has always been socially acceptable for women of all classes to attend football matches. Women too, have always been knowledgeable fans, understanding the intricacies of a complex game.

"You are getting money under false pretences. You don't know the game any more than a baby in arms."

An Essendon lady member to the umpire after he gave a Carlton player a free kick in front of goals, as reported in *Melbourne Punch* in 1908.

At the beginning of the new century, Collingwood created the first ladies' stand. In *Melbourne Punch* it was argued that female fans would be happier separated from the men and the men would be happier being able to talk "in a strain that the gentle Annies wouldn't approve of." These obviously weren't the same gentle Annies that had attacked umpire Roberts with their hat pins!

The Fans

- Each year since 1997, attendances at AFL games have surpassed six million for the year (up to 6.7 million), making it the biggest spectator sport in Australia.
- Rugby league attendances are around three million annually.
- The biggest crowd for an Australian Rules game was 121 696 for the 1970 Grand Final between Collingwood and Carlton at the MCG.
- The biggest football crowd (of any code) in the world was 199 854 people who watched Brazil and Uruguay play soccer in Rio de Janeiro in 1950.
- The AFL grand final is usually the highest rating television sporting event in Australia, in recent years drawing just under three million viewers. This is higher than the audiences for the Melbourne Cup, the opening ceremony for the Olympic Games and the Rugby League grand final. In recent years, however, it has been knocked into second place by the 2003 Rugby World Cup (England vs Australia) and the 2005 Australian Tennis Open final.

1908
1925

The new century dawned and football was as popular as ever. Fans flocked to the game and punters wagered staggering amounts on the final result. Football had prided itself that barristers and barmaids could stand side by side, cheering their team, but the next two decades revealed they didn't exactly see the game in the same way. To the well-to-do, football was a way to create young men with courage, discipline and Christian values. For a lot of the working classes, football was a passion, but it was also a job. Still, the rifts exposed by the squabbles over money were nothing compared to the class divisions exposed by war.

Class Wars

1908 Richmond and University admitted into the VFL.

1911 VFL allows player payments.

1912 Players start to regularly wear numbers on their guernseys and the *Football Record* listing all players is published.

1914 First World War starts.

Last season for University in VFL.

1915 Landing at Gallipoli.

1916 In the VFL, only Collingwood, Richmond, Carlton and Fitzroy continue playing.

The VFA, SANFL, TFL, NTFA suspend playing during the war.

Port Adelaide keep playing and create the Patriotic Football Association.

WAFL vote to suspend play but court rules the decision illegal and competition continues.

1917 Geelong and South Melbourne return to the VFL.

1918 First World War ends.

Seventy-seven VFL players and former players are killed in the First World War.

Essendon and St Kilda return to the VFL.

VFA competition returns.

1919 Melbourne returns to the VFL.

South Australian competition returns.

1920 The Tasmanian competition comes back in full force after being hit by an influenza epidemic the previous season.

1925 North Melbourne, Hawthorn and Footscray move from the VFA to the VFL.

First radio broadcast of a football game.

The great bribery scandal

What would it have been like at the MCG just before the 1910 second semifinal? Imagine that Doug Gillespie wandered into the Carlton change rooms at the MCG with his bag slung over his shoulder. The tang of liniment invaded his nostrils. The mood in the rooms was sombre, but that was to be expected as his team-mates readied themselves for a fierce contest against South Melbourne. As Gillespie dropped his kit on the bench he tried to catch the eye of a mate, but his friend just turned his head away. Finally someone nodded towards the playing list. Gillespie sauntered over to check it out. He wasn't concerned; he was one of the Blues' better players. But, sure enough, he'd been dropped. He couldn't believe it. He tried to ask one of the club administrators what was going on but the man in the suit turned his back on him.

Gillespie wasn't the only player dropped; Doug Fraser and Alex Lang were also omitted. Three of the Blues' best were not going to don the navy blue guernseys that day. The rest of the players were restless, they wanted to know what was going on. In the end it was up to Carlton's revered captain coach Pompey Elliot to address the boys. "It seems," he said from under his magnificent moustache, "the lads have been prepared to sell us out."

It was alleged the omitted players had accepted bribes to play dead, and while nothing was proven the club couldn't chance it. The substitute players, who had been reluctant to replace their mates on the playing list, were convinced to take their places on the field.

Within minutes, without a single radio broadcast or a mobile phone, every one of the 42 000-plus fans at the ground knew what had happened. As the players ran onto the ground, the decimated Blues were cheered and their poor rivals, the Bloods, booed. The Carlton faithful had decided that the villains were not the men who had accepted bribes but the party doing the bribery. Now who would want to bribe the Carlton players into playing poorly? Well surely South Melbourne. Even the South Melbourne supporters appeared to believe their team was guilty of something, sitting quietly while the Blues abused the South Melbourne players.

If there was a match Carlton could throw, this was the one. The Blues were guaranteed a place in the grand final. The Bloods, on the other hand, were playing for survival in the finals. Against the vilification of the crowd, in a spiteful match, the Bloods put in a magnificent effort and won the game.

The aftermath ripped at the heart of the Blues. It was revealed the administrators had been investigating for weeks. They knew players were being offered money to play dead, and could have stepped in before anyone had accepted the bribes. Instead they let it go ahead, testing the players to see what they would do. When the players failed the test and accepted the bribes, they were punished. Some people felt the players had been set up by their own club. The final investigation exonerated Gillespie,

but Lang and Fraser were found guilty and each suspended for 99 weeks.

The scandal sucked energy out of South Melbourne and they were easily overcome by Collingwood the next week. The Pies faced the Blues in the grand final a week later and the Blues lost in a vicious contest that had the newspapers in a flurry.

The Carlton scandal was hardly the first case of bribery in football. Back in 1890 the reverse situation had occurred when there were whispers that several South Melbourne players had accepted bribes to let Carlton win. The investigation didn't find any proof but there were plenty of rumours. And in the VFA grand final in 1902, Richmond players were spotted receiving their pay-off… at three-quarter time.

"Football scandal:
A player approached
'Will you run a bye?'
Sum of £10 Accepted"

Argus newspaper headline, 1910.

Betting had been popular for years and as the wagers grew so did the potential for players to be bribed. What singled out the Carlton bribery scandal from what had come before were the divisions it exposed within the club — divisions between the administrators, often wealthy men of standing, and the players, who were often working class.

The basic wage (the minimum wage a worker could be paid) had been introduced in 1908 and most of Australia had recovered well from the depression, but there was still a gulf between the lifestyles of the wealthy and that of the working classes.

John Wren was a sports promoter and a gambler. In working-class Collingwood, he was legendary but he had plenty of detractors, including Frank Hardy, whose novel Power without Glory *was based on Wren. The book is set in the fictional suburb of Carringbush. Collingwood is now sometimes referred to as Carringbush.*

Football was officially an amateur sport, players playing for the love of the game and a few shillings for expenses, but amateurism was a farce. For years clubs paid generous player 'expenses' and arranged good jobs for their best players. There were rumours Collingwood were paying players with money from infamous Collingwood bookie John Wren. When it was revealed that Essendon had arranged jobs for players, VFL officials were particularly upset. They thought Essendon, a club with upper-class ties, should have defended the values of amateur sportsmanship. And for years players were regularly poached from one club to another with generous offers.

In 1911, Carlton, perhaps still stinging

from their loss in the grand final the year before, proposed the rule prohibiting payment be removed. The vote was carried 19 to one. Football went professional.

East meets West

Match fixing was rarely proven and it wasn't confined to Melbourne or to the players. At the 1905 Grand Final between East Fremantle and West Perth, East Fremantle and their fans cheered and hollered at the end of the game, thinking they had won by a point. But the mood changed quickly when the umpires told the team that the game had in fact been a draw. Six independent newspaper reporters, who had all been keeping their own scores, agreed that East Fremantle had won by a point, but the umpire is always right and a rematch was arranged. Things looked ominous for East Fremantle in the rematch from the start. Despite all the evidence to the contrary, the bookies had West Perth as the favourites. Naive punters must have thought the East Fremantle odds were a godsend and wagered heavily. East Fremantle got a horror

One Geelong player, Stephens, put up a gutsy performance against Fitzroy in 1907 when he kicked five goals. Nothing remarkable about that except that he had been injured in the first quarter and played the last three with his arm in a sling.

run from the umpires, West Perth won by four points… and the bookies cleaned up.

War

At the end of 1914 season, University, a club who had held onto its amateur status in a professional competition, admitted defeat and announced they were withdrawing from the VFL competition. But it was barely front page news. War had just broken out in Europe.

The first game of the 1915 season started just as soldiers were landing at the rugged coastline of Gallipoli. It would take months for the lists of casualties to filter back to Australia. For a few months at least, the country was blissfully ignorant of the tragedy that was taking place on the shoreline of Turkey.

Enlistment poster from the First World War aimed at sportsmen. (Troedel Collection, La Trobe Picture Collection, State Library of Victoria.)

In the early days of the war, patriotic fervour kept spirits up. In support of the war effort, St Kilda changed their colours from red, white and black (German colours) to red, yellow and black (the Belgian flag).

But in football the spectre of war didn't unite people; it exposed prejudices and tensions between the classes. A huge debate raged. Many of the elite believed football existed only to teach young men the values of courage and discipline. In times of war the pigskin should be tossed aside and the rifle taken up in defence of Britain and its allies. Footballers were called "paid gladiators" and "mercenaries". It was even claimed that football was treasonous as it encouraged fit young men to stay at home instead of enlisting. This vitriol was not directed at footballers in general but at what was seen as the scourge of football—professionalism.

University Football Club was formed in 1859 but only played in the VFL between 1908 and 1914. The players were strictly amateur and represented Melbourne University. They required a matriculation certificate or higher degree before they could play for the VFL club. Not surprisingly, they were nicknamed the Students.

The enlistment figures appeared to back their claims. In amateur sporting clubs enlistment was high. In the professional clubs enlistment was low. When the ball was bounced for the start of the 1915 season, only 51 VFA and VFL players had enlisted. This was around 13 per cent of those eligible, well under the 39 per cent national average. But in the professional clubs many more of the players, who also worked as labourers and tradesmen, were married.

But why was football targeted? As one writer to the *Sport* newspaper noted, “It will be observed that the carpers do not attack golf or motoring… where lies the gumption in singling out football as a means of getting something off their chests.” This was now a class war.

The battle to suspend competition failed in the VFL (though only four clubs, all working class, competed in the 1916 competition) but around the country most of the other competitions were suspended.

Supporters too were targeted. They were asked to boycott the game, branded loafers and layabouts if they didn't. A campaign started that featured a soldier standing over his dead mate looking to a vision of football crowd with the caption “Will they never come?” The unthinkable happened — football crowds began to drop off.

Mates and diggers

On the morning of the 1915 Grand Final, the Collingwood secretary, EW ‘Bud’ Copeland, motored out to the training camp in Broadmeadows to pick up his ruck combination, Doc Seddon and Paddy Rowan, for the game. The two men had enlisted but Copeland had worked hard to get permission for them to have leave that day to play.

During the season the Blues had seen the better of the Pies on both occasions, but by a measly point on the first occasion and only double that margin on the second. Paddy

and Doc were crucial to the Pies' line-up if they were going to reverse the trend. Paddy, the slightly taller of the two, took the tap-ins while Doc was a master in clearing space with his elbows and body. Paddy and Doc played footy and cricket together, worked together, and when war came they enlisted together. It was Doc who introduced Paddy to Louise, the woman Paddy would marry. They were as close as two mates could get and it showed on the footy field.

Paddy Rowan's real name was Percy Rowe; he'd changed it when he'd become a boxer. He didn't want his mum to know he was stepping into the ring. When he started playing for Collingwood, he stuck with Paddy.

When Copeland arrived at the barracks, he was horrified to find out his two key men had been sent out on a 10-mile march. (Collingwood legend has it that their commanding officer was a Carlton supporter.) Copeland bundled the two dog-tired players into the car and set out for the MCG.

In 1915 the competition was still at full force and despite the war the grand final crowd was an impressive 39 343. The game was fast and fierce and both teams played with passion and courage. At the third break there was less than a goal between the two teams. Early in the fourth quarter Collingwood hit the front and the fans could see the flag coming back to Victoria Park. But every Pies supporter will tell you that what happened next has since been repeated over and over again; Carlton received a dubious free kick in front of goal. The tide turned and the Collingwood players, perhaps having simply run out of legs, were overrun. The Blues were on song with champion wingman George Challis starring. The final margin of 33 points didn't reflect the closeness of the game and the Blues won their second premiership in succession.

Fitzroy has the unique honour of winning both the wooden spoon and the premiership in the same year. In 1916 they finished on the bottom of the ladder but with only four teams in the competition, they qualified for the finals. They won all their finals matches to run away with the premiership.

When Paddy and Doc went off to war, Paddy's wife, Louise, was pregnant with their first child. But Paddy, like so many of his generation, was killed in Somme, France, and never saw his baby son. Doc came home, and after some time, married Louise and raised his best mate's kid as his own.

Challis too went to Egypt and France. Among all the hysteria about players not doing their duty, Challis—a fit and healthy sportsman—had a hard time trying to enlist.

He was rejected because his toes overlapped. After several attempts he was accepted. But like Paddy he never returned, killed on the French battlefields.

After the war

Despite the rhetoric that labelled footy players traitors, most gave up their match payment of 25 shillings a game during the war years. As the list of dead mates came through day after day, many could barely gather the passion for football but they kept playing believing that they were performing a public service.

Young men started to return from the front. Some were disabled or seriously disfigured by wounds they'd received on the front. Others were suffering shell shock or the effects of gassing. Not all the wounds were physical; many carried emotional scars. Around the country the Red Cross opened convalescent homes, nerve homes and sanatoriums for returning soldiers.

The war finally ended in 1918. When two barrackers were taken to hospital after a brawl between Collingwood and Richmond larrikins, the *Bulletin* newspaper remarked it was "like old times". After the war, people were just happy to be alive and the early 1920s was party time. While flappers — young women who had discarded the moral conventions (and underwear) that had constrained them — were dancing the Charleston and the jitterbug, the new kids on the block, Richmond, were dominating the VFL. The Tigers had been a late addition to the VFL, arriving from the VFA in 1908. In 1920 they won their first VFL flag and followed it up with another a year later. After the 1921 Grand Final, Tiger forward, Barney Herbert, cried out to the fans, "How did we do it?" To which the fans would gloriously announce "Ate 'em alive."

The rivalry between the two Victorian administrations, the VFA and the VFL, continued. When a charity match was organised between Essendon, the VFL premiers in 1924, and the VFA champions Footscray, no one expected Footscray to win. To everyone's surprise Footscray thrashed the Dons. Could Essendon have thrown the game? Certainly champion Essendon player, Fitzmaurice, was suspicious. He later said that, when he had words with the players concerned, he was told "What are you squealing about? You could have been in the cut up." Disgusted, Fitzmaurice left Essendon and went to Geelong where he played in a premiership. Footscray always insisted that the game was on the level.

Up there Cazaly

Roy Cazaly had played for St Kilda for eight years, even becoming the Saint's captain, before he ever pulled on a South Melbourne guernsey. Yet it's hard for any footy fan to imagine him in anything else. Certainly it was while he was wearing the red sash that one of footy's most famous sayings was coined.

Cazaly was a sensational ruckman and a great mark. His South Melbourne team-mates began calling out "Up

there Cazaly" to encourage him to leap higher and higher. Soon the fans picked up on it and it became part of the footy lingo. Aussies all around the country, even those who'd never seen a game of Aussie Rules, could be heard to sing it out as an encouragement. Many years later it would even be heard on the battlefield of the Second World War.

Roy Cazaly was ahead of his time. He was a professional in every sense of the word. As a kid, he'd perfected his ruck work by running full pelt at great gum trees, only swinging and twisting his body out of the way at the last minute to avoid crashing into them. He didn't drink or smoke and was considered a bit of a health nut. He banned the fry-up, and was known to take particular care of his feet, bathing and massaging them after each game. He would say, "A man is only as game as he is fit."

Fearless and highly skilled, he didn't instigate the rough stuff but would put a bloke back in his place if he started it, especially if the aggression was directed at younger players. He said, "A fellow who wants to win by bashing your best players is, in the show-down, chicken-hearted." By the time he'd finished his VFL career he'd played 99 games each for St Kilda and South Melbourne.

After South Melbourne, footy took Cazaly to Tasmania, then back to Melbourne and into coaching. He coached Preston, South Melbourne, Hawthorn and Camberwell and is credited with changing Hawthorn's nickname from the flowery Mayblooms to the much fiercer Hawks.

Roy Cazaly played 410 games in Victoria and Tasmania. He was 58 years old when he played his last game. He was a true football professional.

Fairest and Best

Magarey Medal

The South Australian Magarey Medal has been awarded since 1898 to recognise the fairest and most brilliant player in the South Australian league. William Magarey was chairman of the SAFA.

Players that have won the Magarey more than once are:

4 times: R Ebert.

3 times: T MacKenzie, D Moriarty, L Fitzgerald, L Head, B Robran.

2 times: S Hosking, W Scott, B McGregor, R Quinn, R Hank, HR Phillips, J Deane, G McIntosh, A Jarman, D Squire.

Brownlow Medal

Charles Brownlow, Geelong player and administrator, died in 1924. Only weeks later a medal to honour the fairest and best player for the season in the VFL was proposed. It was to be called the Brownlow Medal.

Players that have won the Brownlow more than once:

3 times: Haydn Bunton Snr, Dick Reynolds, Bob Skilton, Ian Stewart.

2 times: Ivor Warne-Smith, Bill Hutchinson, Roy Wright, Keith Greig, Peter Moore, Greg Williams, Robert Harvey.

Sandover Medal

The Sandover Medal — donated by Perth businessman Alfred Sandover — has been presented to the best player in the West Australian Football League since 1921.

Players that have won it more than once are:

4 times: Bill Walker.

3 times: Haydn Bunton Snr, Merv McIntosh, Graham Farmer, Barry Cable.

2 times: John Leonard, Ian Dargie, Sammy Clarke, Ray Sorrell, Phil Kelly, Stephen Michael, Peter Spencer.

The flappers had their dance cut short when, in 1929, an international depression hit. Thousands of men went 'on the wallaby', wandering the countryside, with a swag on their back, looking for work. Football survived, even prospered, as people went to the footy in droves to take their minds off all the doom and gloom. Surprisingly, the depression signalled the era of superstar players. Some were handsome, some had faces only a mother could love, some were gentlemen, some tough as boot nails, but the fans adored them all. Then, just as things were on the improve, war broke out again.

Champions, Superstars and Brawlers

1929 Wall Street crashes signalling the worldwide depression.

1930 Coulter Law adopted, limiting player payments in the VFL to £3 ($6) a week.

1939 Second World War starts in Europe.

1941 Ron Barassi Snr is one of the 55 VFL footballers killed in the Second World War.

Last grand final played at the MCG until 1946.

1942 The VFA suspend playing for the duration of the war.

United States Army Air Forces (USAAF) move into the MCG and rename it Camp Murphy.

1943 RAAF return to the MCG, use it as a base, and call it Camp Ransford.

1945 Victory over Japan.

1946 Footy returns to the MCG in August.

Regular live radio broadcasts of the finals.

Nuts

The end of the 1920s belonged to Collingwood. Tough and working class, Collingwood folk knew about hard times, and while many of the Pies fans were among the worst hit by the depression you would hardly have known it on the footy field. They dominated the competition like no one had before, playing in all the grand finals from 1925 to 1930, winning the last four on the trot. In 1929, they won every game of the home and away season, a feat not yet repeated.

The team was captained by their astute ruckman Syd Coventry, coached by the coach of all coaches, Jock McHale, and holding down full forward was Syd Coventry's brother, Gordon 'Nuts' Coventry.

Gordon grew up in Diamond Creek, with seven older brothers to harass him. His brothers christened him Nuts, because of his big head. It was one of those nicknames that stuck.

It was fear of his older brothers that got Gordon to Collingwood in the first place. In the early 1920s Collingwood had asked the big kid to come to town for a run with the team at training. (Syd, while older than Gordon, was not to make his debut for Collingwood for a few years yet, so on this occasion Gordon was on his own.) Gordon caught the train from Diamond Creek, butterflies in his stomach the entire trip. When he finally stepped onto the platform at Victoria Park he'd all but convinced himself to catch the next train right back home again. It

was only the fear of the ribbing he'd get from his brothers for chickening out that got him to the ground that night.

Gordon wasn't an instant success. In his first game, those butterflies were back, gnawing at his guts. He only managed one lousy kick. Gordon could kick and mark but he moved like an old bear. He told committee man Bud Copeland he wasn't up to big league football, but Copeland wouldn't listen. At Collingwood, you stuck to your guns and Copeland wasn't prepared to let Gordon accept defeat just yet.

"I saw hundreds of lads having their first League games thereafter, but none was so inglorious as mine."
Gordon Coventry

It was a while before Gordon made it back into the side and unfortunately his second game wasn't much chop either, but his third game was a cracker. He'd been bashed from pillar to post by his opponent but still kicked a bag, five goals, and against Carlton too. He was hooked; he wanted to play in a grand final.

Within a couple of years it was impossible to think of Collingwood without the shy and unassuming Nuts Coventry cemented in at full forward. By the time Gordon retired, he'd played in five premiership teams—it could have easily been six.

Gordon was a strong, solid man with a square jaw who played like he looked; there was nothing flashy about Gordon. He stuck to his task of kicking goals, and no one was better at it than he was. A quiet country boy, he didn't talk it up on the field and had never been reported. That was until a game against Richmond in 1936.

Gordon was playing on Joe Murdoch when Gordon claimed Murdoch punched him on the back of the neck, aiming for a nasty nest of boils. Gordon retaliated and was reported, although most witnesses say he barely connected. It didn't matter. The VFL suspended him for eight games—the rest of the season. What followed became one of football's greatest controversies. There was a public outcry. Football had become the lifeblood of Melbourne and no one took their football more seriously than the Magpies fans. Such was the horror at Gordon's suspension it was even raised in parliament. But even the government couldn't get the VFL to budge and Gordon missed the 1936 Grand Final. Joe Murdoch lived until he was 92 and said he

Gordon Coventry's record of 1299 goals wasn't broken until 1999 when Tony Lockett kicked his 1300th. It was said Gordon wore the same pair of boots for all of his 306 games. Lockett carried his boots in the same Adidas bag for his entire career.

never ceased to regret the incident which he described as the worst day of his life.

Upset and angry Gordon retired, but Collingwood convinced the big man not to go out on such a sour note. He came back for one last season. By the end of his career Gordon had become the first player to kick over 100 goals in a season, the first player to play over 300 games and he kicked a record 1299 goals. Collingwood were well rewarded for sticking with the big kid from Diamond Creek.

Foreign Legion

It was the depression and times were tough, unemployment was high and many families barely had enough to eat. Archie Crofts was doing well; he owned a chain of grocery stores. The Coulter Law had been instigated in the VFL, limiting player payments, but it didn't stop Archie offering interstate players a job if they came and lined up for his beloved South Melbourne.

In Western Australia unemployment was nearly 30 per cent and Archie's offer was irresistible. Some of the greatest players from Western Australia, Tasmania and South Australia came to play for the Blood-stained Angels, South Melbourne. Sports writer Hec de Lacy joked that so many Western Australians had joined South Melbourne, the club should be renamed the Swans, the emblem of Western Australia. And it was.

With all that imported talent, people expected the

glam South Melbourne team to dominate and in 1933, sure enough, they won the premiership. Years later South Melbourne's champion goal kicker, Bob Pratt said, "The 1933 Grand Final was played at the depth of the Great Depression—you wouldn't believe how hard times were: every penny counted. Yet over 75 000 people packed the MCG to see that game; the big majority walked miles to the ground, just to save the train fare. It just shows how much Melbourne people love their football."

In 1934 Bob Pratt kicked 150 goals and the Swans made the grand final, but to everyone's surprise they were overrun on the day by Perc Bentley's Tigers. No matter—they finished the 1935 home and away season on the top of the ladder and won a spot in that year's grand final. The day before the big game against the

Herb 'Wingy' Screaigh played 206 games with East Perth from 1932 to 1946 and represented Western Australia in state football. What made Wingy's achievements particularly spectacular was that he was missing a hand and part of his lower arm. Once, when he first started playing, an opponent appealed for a free kick when Wingy punched the ball with his stump instead of "a clenched fist" as stated in the rules. The umpire, quite rightly, called "play on".

Pies, Pratt stepped off a tram in Prahran and was hit by a truck. Of course everyone assumed the truck driver was a Collingwood supporter, but he was actually a South Melbourne fan. He must have felt sick about it. Pratt was crucial to the Swans and in the end they lost to Collingwood by 20 points with the terrible score line of 7 goals, 16 behinds for 58 points. Pratt recovered and went on to play in the 1936 Grand Final, where once again the Bloods lost to the Pies.

They'd made four grand finals in a row but only managed one flag. For many people, South Melbourne's foreign legion proved the adage "a champion team will always beat a team of champions".

Captain Blood and the shirtfront

On the top of Richmond Hill sits the imposing bluestone church St Ignatius and next to it St Ignatius School. Sport was a serious subject at St Ignatius School. These were the days when it mattered if you were Catholic or Protestant. The two denominations rarely mixed except on the sporting arena. Whether it was cricket or football, on the scoreboard, St Ignatius made sure they proved Catholics were just as good (if not better) than the Protestants.

Jack Dyer's mum sent him to St Ignatius School to see if her gangly son had talent. Turned out he did. St Ignatius's sportsmaster was so impressed that when he was transferred to another school he took Jack with him. But in the depression, school was a luxury, and Jack, like many kids of his generation, had to leave when he was 14 to get a job.

A few years later he was sitting on the Tigers bench. His first game, a bit like Gordon Coventry's, wasn't a raging success but it wasn't long before he was the dominant ruckman of the competition. At 185 cm (6 foot 1 inch) and 88 kg (14 stone) he was a big bloke for the times and he was never reluctant to use his size and strength in play. The football played in the depression, when players were often playing for the only family income, was the toughest football ever played, and Jack Dyer was the toughest footballer of that era. *The Age* newspaper wrote, "Dyer developed a straight-ahead, full-chested rush that has no counter." If he didn't invent the shirtfront, Jack Dyer certainly perfected it. To the opposition supporters Dyer was a loathsome brute, but to every Tiger fan he was the greatest champion of them all. He was also the epitome of Richmond: hard, even brutal, but rarely without a grin on his face.

In 1936 Errol Flynn was setting the girls' hearts a flutter with his Hollywood charms. When his swashbuckling pirate movie *Captain Blood* hit the screens, it didn't take long for someone to think the way Errol butchered his foe on the screen was reminiscent of the way Dyer decimated his opponents. 'Captain Blood' became arguably the most famous nickname in footy.

Dyer lived up to his nickname, poleaxing many opponents, but perhaps because of his infamy, Dyer's

legacy to football is sometimes forgotten. He played 312 games for Richmond between 1931 and 1949 and continued as a non-playing coach until 1952. He played in two premiership teams and despite all the hype was only reported a couple of times and suspended once in his long career. He is also credited with inventing the drop punt. He said he picked it up from the Collier brothers from Collingwood, who used it as a way of lobbing the ball over an opponent's head to one another. Dyer recognised its accuracy and began to use it for distance.

"But I wasn't the sort [to win a Brownlow]. I had lots of rough edges. Brownlow medallists don't have edges; they're all smooth…"

Jack Dyer talking to Neil Kearney.

In the 1930s football was professional, but payments were limited by the Coulter Law. Life was tough if you were living on your football wages. Players, who could find other work, did. Captain Blood was a policeman when he wasn't contesting the bounce of the ball and kicking goals. Years later, after he'd finished coaching, Dyer tried his hand in the media. He wrote a footy column, "Dyer'ere", commentated games on radio, and later created havoc on Channel 7 with Lou Richards and Bobbie Davis. He was one of the first ex-footy players to become a media star. Dyer's success was particularly fascinating. He had a way with words — an unusual way. His humorous quips became known as Dyerisms.

A few Dyerisms:

"If you don't mind, umpire!"
"He's a good ordinary footballer." (Talking about Carlton sensation Peter Bosustow.)
"A champion team will always beat a team of champions unless the team of champions is very, very good."
"Mark Lee's long arms reaching up like giant testicles."
"I want you to pair off in threes."

Pastor Doug

It was 1914. The men of Cummeragunja reserve had been sent away to cut timber, leaving the women and children alone, when the police arrived without warning. Some of the girls knew what was happening. They ran for the river, dived in and swam away. A copper grabbed Doug Nicholls's sister and dragged her to the police car. Nicholls's mother tried to stop him, but she wasn't strong enough. The car drove off, leaving Nicholls's mother, Florence, wailing.

Nicholls's sister was forcibly removed from her family as part of the government policy to raise Aboriginal children in white communities. Now known as the Stolen Generation, these children grew up without their relatives or culture. Florence was devastated by the loss

of her daughter. Years later Nicholls described the police that day as "gutless wonders". In the early part of the 20th century life was particularly cruel if you were black. Nicholls was an eight-year-old kid, small for his age, when his sister was taken away. That same year he left school to find work.

For years after that day, Nicholls made a living working as a labourer around country Victoria. He also played a bit of country footy. Nicholls quickly realised that there was one way a black man like himself might find reasonable employment and respect within the white community, and that was through sport. He was only 157 cm (5 foot 2 inches) tall, but he was fast, nimble and had a sensational leap.

In the 1920s, Nicholls headed down to Melbourne to try his chances in the big league. He got himself a job at the fruit and veg market sweeping up, kipping under the trestle tables at night. He tried out with Carlton, performing well and surviving every cull of the list until the final cut. Too small was the official excuse, but Nicholls was convinced his team-mates were not happy about playing with an Aboriginal and had complained he smelled.

Northcote, in the VFA, didn't suffer from such prejudices. They gave the little wingman a run and the team was so impressed with his first game they took up a collection to supplement his playing fee. Doug Nicholls played for Northcote for the next five years, earning money playing football in the winter and as a professional runner in the summer. The prize money went as quickly as he won it, on flashy clothes and parties. Nicholls lived the high life.

Then in 1931 Jimmy Sharman's Boxing Troupe came to town. On the stage stood six or seven men in their colourful robes. On their feet they wore laced-up boots. The pennants fluttered in the wind as the crowd were coaxed to challenge one of Jimmy's men to a boxing match. It was just a few days before Northcote were to take on Oakleigh in the grand final but Nicholls was game. He went into the ring twice, winning both bouts. No doubt Nicholls's coach would have been horrified if he'd known. Northcote didn't take the flag that year but Nicholls was widely thought to be best on ground. But Jimmy Sharman offered Nicholls a lucrative contract. This was the depression and the offer was too good to refuse. It looked like Doug Nicholls was lost to football forever when he went on the road with Sharman and his boxers. But Fitzroy had other ideas.

Nicholls was only seven months into his contract with Jimmy when a couple of men from Fitzroy travelled to NSW to make Nicholls a generous offer. It was tempting but Nicholls wouldn't break his contract with Sharman. But the showman must have been a footy fan because he let Nicholls out of his contract so the little wingman could become a Maroon.

Nicholls's time at Fitzroy was a dramatic contrast to the bad experience he had at Carlton. He was respected and admired both as a player and a man. Doug had found

religion, and after one game his team-mates presented him with a Bible as a symbol of how they accepted both him and his religious beliefs.

Doug Nicholls became a social worker and pastor, working with the Aboriginal community, particularly around Fitzroy. He was named Victorian Father of the Year in 1962, was the first Aboriginal to be knighted in 1972 and was made Governor of South Australia in 1976.

For six years Nicholls occupied centre wing at Fitzroy. He picked up a best and fairest and was the first Aboriginal to represent Victoria in an interstate game. Then in 1939 he told his coach he couldn't continue in the finals. He'd been carrying a bung knee for some time, but now his eyesight was going. Blighted by trachoma, he couldn't judge the flight of the ball as he once had. He stepped out of football but it was only the start of another life for him.

Hollywood star

In the era of great movie stars, Haydn Bunton was as good looking as any Hollywood idol. It was said he even ironed his shoelaces before running out to play.

Haydn came to Melbourne from Albury as a teenager and was much sought after, especially by Carlton and Fitzroy. Fitzroy beat Carlton in the fierce bidding. A disgruntled Carlton dobbed in Fitzroy to the VFL for breaking the Coulter Law and Haydn sat out 1930 as punishment. But when he did play his first game in 1931, unlike Coventry and Dyer, he had no problem hitting his straps, he was best on ground. He won the Brownlow in his first year. He would go on to win two more. Fitzroy were not the strong team they had been earlier in the century (in the first 26 years of the VFL, Fitzroy won seven flags) but Haydn provided the fans with plenty of entertainment. He gained the respect and admiration of the opposition. Dyer and Pratt were both fans.

Haydn was the ultimate sportsman, athletic, graceful, fearless, and a gentleman of the highest order. After his experience at Carlton, Doug Nicholls would change in a corner away from the other players. When Nicholls went to Fitzroy, Haydn asked him why he would change alone and Nicholls simply said, "Ah well, you know how it is." From then on Bunton, the club's greatest player, would always change next to Nicholls to remind everyone Nicholls was part of the team.

For years the VFL had been ruthlessly raiding the other states for their star players. In the late 1930s the wheel turned when the WAFL started targeting VFL players. Bunton was one of the players who moved across the continent. He played for Subiaco winning three Sandover Medals to match his Brownlows. Bunton has a fair claim to being one of the most skilled players ever to pull on a pair of footy boots. Despite his stellar career, Bunton only

played in one grand final, for Port Adelaide in 1945. They lost.

For several years after that, Haydn—the player umpires respected—became a man in white himself. Not surprisingly, he excelled as an umpire.

When he left football, Haydn devoted himself to his family. Haydn Bunton's son, Haydn Bunton Jnr, was struck down with a crippling childhood hip disease. Haydn Snr dedicated himself to his son and helped to rehabilitate him. The end of Haydn Bunton Snr's life was tragic. His wife died unexpectedly on Christmas day 1954, six months later he was fatally injured in a car accident.

Haydn Bunton Jnr went on to become a champion footballer in his own right, and while he never played VFL, he followed his father's legacy by winning the Sandover Medal.

Bluey

A week before the start of the 1939 finals series, prime minister Robert Menzies declared Australia was at war with Germany.

For football, things were very different from the First World War. St Kilda kept their colours, and while the VFA, South Australian and Tasmanian competitions were suspended, there was never any real attempt to stop football being played by the VFL or WAFL. It was thought important to keep morale up and to do that those left in Australia should keep the 'home fires burning'. No longer did people think football existed just to teach young men skills to be used on the battlefield. Clinton Wines, a Carlton player who fought in the Second World War, made it clear when asked to compare war and football. He said, "War is a far grimmer business."

Keith 'Bluey' Truscott joined the RAAF to become a fighter pilot. He had been a member of Melbourne's winning 1939 and 1940 premiership teams. As a fighter pilot, he fought in the Battle of Britain and the Battle of Milne Bay. He had victories over 15 German aircraft and further victories against the Japanese.

In 1942, Bluey was in Melbourne on his way to the Pacific conflict after returning from England. On impulse he rang his old coach, 'Checker' Hughes, and asked for a game that Saturday. Hughes was delighted to have his old half forward flanker back.

As Bluey ran onto the ground the hysteria was contagious. Fans engulfed him. Boys in their knee-length shorts, men with their ties knotted tightly under their collars and their hair slicked down with brilliantine, and ladies in their floral dresses and sensible lace-up shoes, all wanted to touch Bluey. As Richmond's Jack Dyer grabbed Bluey and pushed him towards the usually one-eyed Tiger fans, a glorious cheer rang out.

Melbourne were always going to find the game hard going, more than any other club they had been depleted by the war. Richmond was well ahead when Jack Dyer surprisingly (and purposely) dropped a mark in Melbourne's goal square; Bluey grabbed the loose ball and kicked a goal. The crowd was ecstatic.

The next day Bluey met his old headmaster and test cricketer Bill Woodfull in the street and Woodfull asked Bluey how he had enjoyed the game. "Not for me," replied Bluey, "too dangerous." Bluey died the next year in an aircraft accident.

Changi Brownlow

Peter Chitty had played for St Kilda before he enlisted. When Singapore fell in 1942, Chitty was captured and sent to the infamous Changi prison camp. Tens of thousands of prisoners were locked up at Changi. In the early days the Japanese provided basic rice rations and little else. Starvation and dysentery were the biggest problems facing the prisoners at Changi. To supplement their diet they grew their own vegetables, and to take their minds off their rumbling bellies they

It wasn't just at home that footy was keeping up morale—one thousand footballs were sent to Libya for the troops.

entertained themselves by putting on shows and staging a six-team football competition. Wild pigs were caught to get bladders for the footballs, which were made from boot leather, and rubber trees made perfect goalposts. Wilfred 'Chicken' Smallhorn had played for Fitzroy; in Changi he was the umpire. Chitty captained 'Victoria' to a win over 'The Rest' at the beginning of 1943. Before the match, Chitty was presented with the Changi Brownlow. It was the only one ever awarded. Afterwards a new Japanese commander banned football and set the men to work seven days a week.

Bloodbath

There was dancing in the streets when victory over Japan was announced in August 1945, but a few weeks later if you'd watched the 1945 Grand Final you would have thought war was still being waged. What should have been the victory grand final was a vicious and violent battle which would become known as the infamous 'Bloodbath'.

Somehow 63 000 people wedged themselves into Princes Park, a ground with a capacity of only 43 000, because the RAAF were still stationed at the MCG. The two coaches that day were Perc Bentley for the Blues and 'Bull' Adams for South Melbourne. The two hard nuts were Bob Chitty, the Carlton captain, and Jack 'Basher' Williams for the Swans.

The first quarter was reasonably calm. Carlton was ahead by a couple of goals when the Swans kicked poorly.

Then in the second the Swans surged ahead with a couple of good goals. It was then that Chitty took action. He'd always contended that the best way to unsettle a team was to deck one of their young players. "They forget everything and lose their self-control. It's a waste of time hitting an old pro..." he said. When 17-year-old Ron Clegg was felled by Chitty, that's exactly what happened; the Swans lost sight of the ball as they went looking for a brawl. Chitty kept his mind on the task at hand, unnerving the opposition. "There's only one thing that gets them madder than belting a kid and that's belting a little guy," he said. Down went Swans' rover, Billy Williams. In retribution the Swans went after Carlton rookie Ken Hands. The umpire spotted Hands lying unconscious on the ground. Next to him stood Jack Williams, hands on hips. The crowd, who until then had been perhaps a little astonished and embarrassed at what was happening on the field, went ballistic. Bottles were thrown onto the ground and at one point police had to break up the clash between players, trainers, ambulance men and officials. Later in the match, Chitty, who had been the villain, was poleaxed. He

Carlton toughman Bob Chitty played the role of Ned Kelly in the 1951 movie The Glenrowan Affair.

recovered, kicked the goal that sealed the match for the Blues, and turned hero.

In the end, 16 charges were laid against 10 players, seven of whom were suspended for periods ranging from four weeks to a whole season. Chitty got eight weeks, Williams, 12.

One of the blokes suspended was Carlton's Fred Fitzgibbon. Fitzgibbon wasn't actually playing in the grand final, having been suspended the week before for striking in the preliminary final against Collingwood (a game that some say was even more brutal than the grand final). Fitzgibbon, sitting in the crowd, had jumped the fence and entered the fray. He was found guilty of brawling and suspended for a further four matches.

Nicknames

Here are just a few of the more famous player nicknames.

Nickname	*Player*	*Clubs*
Basher	Jack Williams	South Melbourne
Big Nick	John Nicholls	Carlton
Bluey	Keith Truscott	Melbourne
	Frank Adams	Melbourne
	Guy McKenna	West Coast Eagles
Buddha	Garry Hocking	Geelong
Butch	Alan Gale	Fitzroy
Bull	Bill Adams	Fitzroy, Melbourne
	Alan Richardson	Richmond, South Melbourne
Bulldog	Kevin Murray	Fitzroy
Captain Blood	Jack Dyer	Richmond
Checker	Frank Hughes	Richmond, Melbourne (coach)
Chicken	Wilfred Smallhorn	Fitzroy
Chimp	Bob Skilton	South Melbourne

Nickname	***Player***	***Clubs***
Crackers	Peter Keenan	Melbourne, North Melbourne, Essendon
Cowboy	Kevin Neale	St Kilda
Diesel	Greg Williams	Geelong, Sydney, Carlton
Disco	Michael Roach	Richmond
Dominator	Wayne Johnston	Carlton
Doc	Darrel Baldock	St Kilda
EJ / Mr Football	Ted Whitten	Footscray
Fish	Paul Salmon	Essendon, Hawthorn
Flea	Dale Weightman	Richmond
Flying Dutchman	Paul van der Haar	Essendon
Flying Doormat	Bruce Doull	Carlton
General	Mark Lee	Richmond
Ghost	Jim Jess	Richmond
Geelong Flier/Woofa	Bob Davis	Geelong
Galloping Gasometer	Mick Nolan	North Melbourne
God	Gary Ablett	Hawthorn, Geelong
Harry	Justin Madden	Essendon, Carlton
Hungry	Kevin Bartlett	Richmond
Incredible Hulk	Rene Kink	Collingwood, Essendon, St Kilda

Nickname	*Player*	*Clubs*
Jerker	Graeme Jenkin	Collingwood, Essendon
Kid / Hood	Dermott Brereton	Hawthorn, Sydney, Collingwood
The King / Duck	Wayne Carey	North Melbourne, Adelaide
King Richard	Dick Reynolds	Essendon
Knuckles	Neil Kerley	West Adelaide, Glenelg
Lethal / Barney	Leigh Matthews	Hawthorn
Mad Dog	Robbie Muir	St Kilda
Macedonian Marvel	Peter Daicos	Collingwood
Nipper	James Bradford	Collingwood, North Melbourne
Nuts	Gordon Coventry	Collingwood
Ox	David Schwarz	Melbourne
Pebbles	Anthony Rocca	Sydney, Collingwood
Piggy	Jason Dunstall	Hawthorn
Plough	Terry Wallace	Hawthorn, Richmond, Footscray
Plugger	Tony Lockett	St Kilda, Sydney
Polly	Graham Farmer	Geelong
Rat	John Platten	Hawthorn
Rocket	Rodney Eade	Hawthorn, Brisbane

Nickname	Player	Clubs
Sam	John Newman	Geelong
Skinny	Jack Titus	Richmond
Sticks	Stephen Kernahan	Carlton
Smokey	Ron Clegg	South Melbourne
Soapy	Harry Vallence	Carlton
SOS (Son of Serge)	Stephen Silvagni	Carlton
Spider	Peter Everitt	St Kilda, Hawthorn
Spud	Danny Frawley	St Kilda
Tiger	Brent Crosswell	Carlton, North Melbourne, Melbourne
Turk	Tommy Lahiff	Essendon, South Melbourne, Hawthorn
Twiggy	Ross Dunne	Collingwood
Whale	Brian Roberts	Richmond, South Melbourne
Wow	Warren Jones	Carlton, St Kilda
Yabby	Allan Jeans	St Kilda, Hawthorn (coach)

Yes Coach

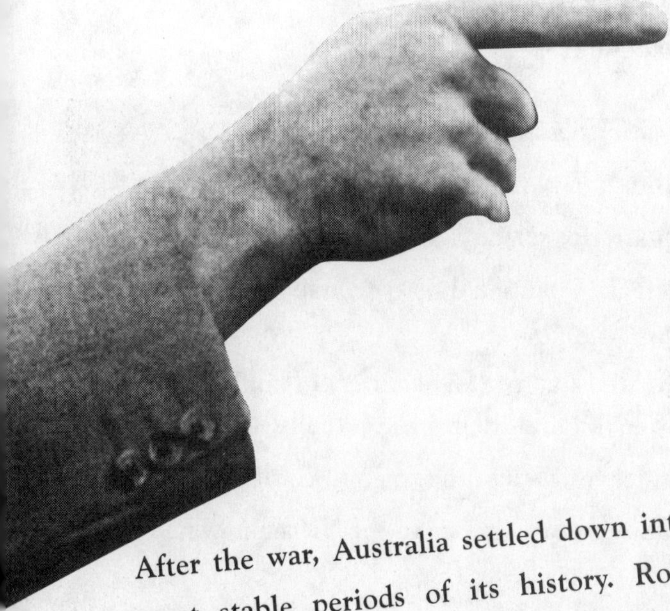

After the war, Australia settled down into one of the most stable periods of its history. Robert Menzies became prime minister for the second time in 1949 and remained in the top job until 1966. Australia was conservative and so was football. The popularity of the game increased and the VFL decided not to meddle with the winning formula. In the 1950s and 1960s the great coaches reigned, their teams settled on top and were hardly ever knocked off.

1949	Robert Menzies elected prime minister.
1956	Television arrives in Australia.
1957	Last quarter of selected match televised live.
1961	Live telecasts banned due to drop in attendances at games.
1962	VFL buys 212 acres (86 hectares) of land in Mulgrave to build their own football stadium.
1965	Barassi leaves Melbourne to go to Carlton.
	Australia commits troops to the Vietnam War.

See the Bombers fly

Australia's middle class prospered after the war and so did the club with a traditionally middle-class supporter base—Essendon. They played in every grand final from 1946 to 1951, walking away with three flags, although most Essendon supporters would have thought it should have been more.

Essendon had seen off Melbourne for the 1946 flag and were determined to make it two in a row in 1947, in their match against Carlton. Fans started queuing up well in advance to get tickets. The parkland around the MCG became a small camp city as mad fans marked out their spot in the queue. At night they built bonfires and had singalongs. The arduous task of getting a ticket meant the grand final crowds of the 1940s and 1950s were all dedicated supporters, and the atmosphere within the MCG was electric. That year Essendon led most of the day but never by much more than a few goals. They just couldn't shake Carlton. With only five points the difference, and a few minutes to play, the ball found its way down to the Blues' forward line where first-year player Fred Stafford was having, until then, an average game. He gathered the loose ball and kicked a goal with his left foot. A few moments later the siren sounded, Carlton had won by a point and Stafford had written himself into the history books. The Essendon players fell to the ground, many so devastated they cried.

Essendon had another gut-wrenching year in 1948

when they played Melbourne for the flag. Every Bomber fan must have been cursing as the team kicked atrociously. When the final siren sounded the scores were level although the Bombers had 15 more shots on goal. In the replay the next week, they lost momentum and the flag.

In 1949 Essendon had a new recruit at full forward. The Bombers already had two legends in the team: Dick Reynolds and Bill Hutchinson. Now they added a third. John Coleman kicked 12 goals in his first game. That year Essendon exacted some revenge on Carlton for their loss two years earlier. They annihilated the Blues in the grand final and in the end the only point of interest was whether Coleman would kick a ton in his first year. He went into the final quarter still needing four goals to make a hundred. The fans were on the edge of their seats as he managed one, two and then three. But it looked like the last would evade him as the time for the final siren to sound drew near. Then with only minutes to go, he kicked a fourth and made his ton.

The medal awarded to the player who kicks the greatest number of goals in the AFL home and away season is called the Coleman Medal. The medal was called the Leading Goalkicker Medal until 1954, but from 1955 it honoured John Coleman.

Coleman was a goal-kicking freak and fans would change ends each quarter just so they could get a better look at the great man in action. In 1950—his second year—Coleman kicked 120 goals.

In 1951 Coleman missed the grand final in a controversial incident. In the last game of the home and away season, Carlton's Harry Caspar hit Coleman and Coleman retaliated. These facts have never been disputed.

In the 1950s there were some interesting ideas on nutrition and fitness. Ken McKaige played for Melbourne and Carlton and tells how he would eat steak and eggs before the game and have a lit cigarette brought out to him on the ground by the trainer during breaks in play.

Both were reported by the goal umpire and found themselves at the tribunal the next Tuesday night. Carlton was not in the finals, but Essendon were favourites to collect themselves another flag. Fans gathered outside the tribunal offices to hear the verdict. When Caspar got four weeks, the Bomber fans were hopeful. Surely Coleman, as the one who'd retaliated, could only expect half the sentence of the instigator, they reasoned. They should have remembered what had happened to George Coulthard and Gordon Coventry all those years ago. Coleman got four weeks. His punishment was in a sense greater

than Caspar's as his four games would be mostly finals. As Coleman tried to leave the tribunal, tears welling in his eyes, the angry crowd jostled him, knocking him off his feet and he hit his head. Essendon got into the grand final but they lost to Geelong. No Bomber fan has ever doubted that they would have won with Coleman in the side.

Coleman only played 98 games. A career-ending knee injury stopped his record at 537 goals. He did go on to coach the Bombers, exacting revenge on Carlton yet again when they beat the Blues for the flag in 1962.

Mr Football

Like heaps of kids on their block, Ted Whitten and his brother played with a football made out of wrapped-up newspapers. That was until their dad told the two boys that when they could kick the thing 36 metres (40 yards) he'd buy them a proper leather football. Day after day they'd drag him out to the street to measure their kicks until the magical 40 yards had been reached.

By the time he was 17, Ted's practice with the paper footy was paying off, he was training with Footscray and had made the team list, but selection in the senior team was no certainty. The next Thursday night he huddled around the radio with his family eagerly waiting to hear if he'd made the senior list. Finally the announcer read out "centre half-forward… Whitten". Ted was a league footballer.

Ted is one of the few players who can claim he kicked a goal with his first kick in VFL footy, and he is also one of the few players not to hear the final siren in their first game. He was wiped out by his Richmond opponent and carted off to hospital. Apparently fearless, or perhaps a little stupid, Ted got knocked out a lot in his early days. Once he collided with his own ruckman and ended up in a coma. That's when Footscray's coach, the great Charlie Sutton, decided enough was enough and taught Ted how to toughen up. It was good training; Ted became renowned for his courage on the field.

Ted loved the Doggies and he loved playing for the Big V—Victoria. At training one day, Ted slipped back into his old habit of not protecting himself and ended up in the Footscray and District hospital with a black eye after a nasty collision with one of his own team. A specialist checked him out and told him not to play the next week or he might risk permanent damage. But Ted also knew he was up for state selection. He'd been told all he had to do was play well against the Swans that week and he was a certainty. Footscray left the decision up to him. In his own words he "decided to give it a go." Ted went in a little tentatively in the first quarter but as the game went on he resumed his normal playing style—headfirst. Sure enough, he soon collided heavily with a South defender, Keith Browning.

"My head felt as if it had exploded, as searing pain shot through me," said Ted later. "As I wobbled around waiting

for the stars to clear, I realised with relief that Browning had caught me in the good eye." He might have had two black eyes but he also had what he wanted—state selection.

Ted was just a kid from the western suburbs but he had friends in high places. Football was still a great leveller. He had been called up for national service but the army agreed he could have leave to play one game in three. Footscray made the finals in 1951 but Ted's leave wasn't granted. He was devastated. That was until the prime minister, Robert Menzies, stepped in. Ted played and although the Doggies lost, he said "It was an awe-inspiring occasion to run on to a field in one's first league final."

Ted was one of football's great characters, he let his emotions flow freely on the field, gesturing wildly if he thought the umpire's decision was bogus, and later when he coached, inspiring his team with passionate speeches. He was also a bit of a lair. Ted was captain one day when the Doggies played the Swans. Ted jogged to the middle of the ground to face the opposing captain and his good mate, Bob Skilton, for the coin toss. Skilton was a footballer's footballer, a rover of such skill and courage he would go on to win three Brownlows and his club's best and fairest an amazing eight times. As the umpire tossed the coin, Ted called heads and then before the umpire could retrieve the coin ran down the field directing his team to kick with aid of a hefty wind. Skilton and the man in white were left standing bewildered in the centre, neither man exactly sure what had just happened and whether Ted had actually won the toss at all.

For thousands of supporters Ted, or EJ as he was known, was Footscray. He was there when Footscray won their first (and so far, only) premiership in 1954. And when midway through 1957 Charlie Sutton was sacked, Ted, with Sutton's approval, became playing coach. He played 321 games for the club and coached 228.

1954 *Footy Record* (AFL).

Wogs

Melbourne in the 1950s was not the place it is today; it wasn't even the place it had been in the 1880s. There were only a few restaurants in town, the pubs closed at six o'clock and you couldn't get a decent cup of coffee anywhere. Married women were expected to stay home. If you worked for a bank, you had no choice—when you got married, you had to leave. On Sunday the family went to church and had a roast dinner when they got home. Life was a bit boring. Thank goodness for the football.

After the Second World War a large number of Europeans jumped on ships and headed to Australia. It was a long, arduous journey that often ended at Port Melbourne docks. For many years Australia had what was called the 'White Australia' policy which favoured immigration from certain countries, primarily Britain and then other European countries. In the 1950s assimilation was also the policy. New migrants were expected to shed their cultures and languages. Despite the low unemployment rate, many Australians were convinced their jobs were at risk from immigrants and they weren't particularly welcoming. Because Italy had been an enemy during the war, Italian migrants were given a particularly hard time. Italian kids were taunted and called 'wogs'.

Tony Ongarello was good-looking, Italian and he played full forward for Fitzroy. He was a fabulous mark, if not the best set shot for goal. He was the last player to use the place kick in the VFL (where you put the ball on the ground before kicking it). His good looks got him a job on television. By 1955 the largest group of foreign-born residents in Fitzroy were not from Britain but from Italy. Tony became an icon to the Fitzroy Italian community. He was someone they could relate to and he brought a whole new batch of fans to Australian football.

At Carlton, a couple of stocky cousins arrived at Princes Park in the late 1950s. They were John Benetti and Sergio Silvagni. The recruiters were amused by the pair of Italian cousins — until they started to play. Benetti went on to play 88 games for the Blues, Silvagni 239. Silvagni's son, Stephen, followed in his father's footsteps and racked up over 300 games for Carlton.

Fitzroy and Carlton were the suburbs where European migrants settled. The two football clubs simply reflected that change in their playing list. By the late 1960s and early 1970s names like Jesaulenko, Kekovich and Catoggio were commonplace.

The disciplinarian

Norm Smith was a man of principle. It is hard to think of another football identity who upheld the ideals of discipline and fair play like Smith. Smith used football to create good men, not just good footballers.

Smith had been a champion player for Melbourne and Fitzroy but it is as master coach he is best remembered. He coached Fitzroy for a couple of years before moving to Melbourne where he took them from last position in 1951 to play in 11 consecutive finals series between 1954 and 1964, winning six premierships.

When Ron Barassi Snr, a Melbourne premiership player, was killed in the Second World War, Smith became a surrogate father to Ron Jnr. No doubt Smith had a hand in getting the young Barassi to Melbourne in 1953, but once he was there he certainly didn't favour the kid. "Special favours? You're kidding. I had to read the paper to find out if I had got a game, and I was living with the man," said Barassi. Smith said he was probably harder on Barassi

than the other players. When the runner was sent out to deliver messages to Barassi from the coach, the hot-tempered Barassi would often send the runner back with his own two-word response. Luckily for Barassi the runner stuck to the 'runner's code' which states, "I'm only paid to bring the messages out, not to take them back" or no doubt Barassi would have been warming the bench.

Norm Smith was in charge and the players knew it. If you turned up to training with anything like a beard, you were sent home to shave it off. But Smith was also an innovative coach, committed to fast play and moving the ball quickly. He built teams from young men. In 1960 Smith wrote about developing youth and the trend towards height and pace in the game. "I think all players should be developed along individual lines and encouraged to develop their natural style of play while being integrated into a team."

"Mateship is the greatest of all morale builders. Many teams are inclined to forget there's a warm and human side to footy."

Norm Smith, 1960.

The medal awarded to the best player in the VFL/AFL grand final is called the Norm Smith Medal.

As the Melbourne team continued to dominate, Smith insisted that his young players be humble in victory and gracious in defeat. "I know people thought we were elitists or smart-arses," said Melbourne player 'Bluey' Adams, "but I don't think we were, purely because Smithy wouldn't let us be."

Croweater glory

The great rivalry between the Croweaters (South Australia) and the Big V continued throughout the decade. The South Australians had never accepted that the Victorian competition was superior and the interstate clashes had special meaning for them. No more than for Fos Williams. Williams is Port Adelaide's most famous son, coaching the club to nine premierships (six as playing coach). He helped make the Port Adelaide Magpies the most successful senior club in Australia.

In 1963 Williams took his South Australians across the border to face the Victorians on their home turf, the MCG. They hadn't beaten the Big V in Melbourne since 1926. As this was VFL versus SANFL, rather than State of Origin, it meant players like Graham 'Polly' Farmer, a Western Australian who was playing in the VFL, were allowed to play for Victoria. Coached by Bob Davis and captained by Bobby Skilton, the Victorian team reads like a who's who of football. Skilton was one of four players in the side who would later go on to be awarded Legend status in the AFL's Hall of Fame. The others were Ron Barassi and two of the greatest ruckmen the game has ever seen, John Nicholls and Polly Farmer. The Victorians

also boasted Kevin Murray, Darrel Baldock and Sergio Silvagni in their line up.

No one gave the South Australians much hope against the champion-packed Victorian team. But with Neil Kerley and John Cahill in their side, the South Australians had come to play. All around the ground the contest was hard and close, giving the 59 000 fans their money's worth. South Australia's ruckman Bill Wedding held his own all day against Farmer and Nicholls and in the end the margin was only seven points, in favour of the South Australians.

The medal awarded to the best South Australian player in a state game is called the Fos Williams Medal. The medal awarded to the best player in the SANFL grand final is called the Jack Oatey Medal. Jack Oatey was SA's other famous coach and he is credited with the invention of what he called the backscrew punt—otherwise known as the checkside punt, banana or boomerang kick.

It was hailed as the day South Australian football came of age and when the team arrived back in Adelaide, 8000 people came out in the rain to meet them, hurling streamers and letting off firecrackers. Fos Williams later said, "The win is the climax to my football career."

Breen's point

Every kid who has ever kicked a Sherrin around

the backyard has imagined themselves kicking the winner in the dying minutes of the grand final. Barry Breen realised that dream.

In nearly 70 years of league football St Kilda had never tasted grand final success. They'd made the grand final in 1965 but were overrun by Coleman's Bombers. In 1966 they faced up to Collingwood in the last game of the season. The game was a heart stopper all day; four points the difference at quarter time, a point at half-time, four points at three-quarter time. With only minutes to play, the scores were level. What happened next is best described by the two commentators that day, Alan 'Butch' Gale and Mike Williamson.

Gale: "This is madness — they're all on the ball."

Williamson: "Potter has it, he can't break clear, it's taken by Breen… It's a… point, it's a point, St Kilda in front, St Kilda in front."

Gale: "How long have they been playing Mike?"

Williamson: "They have been playing, if my hand will stop shaking and I can see the watch, 27 and a half minutes."

(The Magpies cleared from full back but St Kilda's Bob Murray marks.)

Williamson: "There's Murray's kick to the wing position the outer side… there's the siren! St Kilda have won it! They've won it!"

Gale: "By one point though Mike… I'm shaking."

Williamson: "Butch, I just put the lighted end of a cigarette into my mouth… Oh golly!"

Eighteen-year-old Barry Breen's point had won St Kilda their one and only flag. Captain Darrel 'Doc' Baldock said his lasting memory is of ageing fans coming up to him after the victory, tears streaming down their faces, and saying, "Now I can die happy."

Polly

Graham 'Polly' Farmer grew up near Perth in a home run by a nun, Sister Kate. Unlike Doug Nicholls's sister, Polly wasn't taken from his family forcibly. His single mum put him in the home voluntarily, because she was worried she couldn't take care of her son by herself. At night Polly slept with his football. During the day there would have been no shortage of kids at the home to play kick to kick. His love for footy led Polly into the WAFL and he became East Perth's leading ruckman, playing with the club from 1953 until he moved to Victoria, winning three Sandover Medals while he was there.

Polly was ahead of his time; he created tough training regimes for himself when other players thought training was a bit of a run and a kick of the footy. He perfected the art of body-on-body contact, holding his feet while his opponents rarely held theirs. Polly changed the way the game was played. He was famous for pulling the ball out of the ruck and handballing into space where his rover could collect it on the run, speeding up the pace of the game.

In the early 1960s Polly travelled across the continent to play for Geelong. He was one of the Cats' best in the

1963 Grand Final. And while he played, the Cats never missed the finals. His clashes with John 'Big Nick' Nicholls were legendary. Years on, many people, including champion ruckman John 'Sam' Newman, still credit Polly as the greatest ruckman they ever saw.

Polly played his last game for the Cats in the 1967 Grand Final. That same year a national referendum saw an overwhelming majority of people agree that Australia should change the constitution to allow the federal government to make laws specifically related to indigenous Australians and to override discriminatory state laws. This was a huge result for indigenous Australia. Life for many Aborigines hadn't improved much since Doug Nicholls had kicked the footy around, and in the 1960s you could still count the number of Aboriginal players in the VFL on one hand. But things were beginning to change.

"Graham 'Polly' Farmer is without doubt the best, and hardest to beat, ruckman I have ever played against."
John Nicholls, 1977.

Handball, handball, handball

If Ted Whitten was Footscray, then Ron Barassi was Melbourne. He was part of six Melbourne premiership teams. But Barassi wanted to coach,

and he couldn't see that happening while the legendary Norm Smith was at the helm at Melbourne.

In 1964 Carlton pulled off the coup of the decade when they signed Barassi as their captain coach. Melbourne supporters were devastated. They burned their Barassi guernseys in disgust. Barassi's deal with Carlton was one of the first big salaries in football. His weekly wage was around five times the average earnings at the time and around 10 times what the average footballer earned.

It was only a year after Barassi jumped ship that Melbourne tried to give Norm Smith the boot. In 1965, a year after he'd led the Demons to yet another premiership, Smith was sacked from Melbourne, to the horror of football fans everywhere. Smith, wearing his trademark raincoat, had been the figurehead of the club and had had great success. No one could believe it. It was a scandal. The fallout was huge and he was eventually reinstated, although his relationship with the Demons never fully recovered and he eventually moved on to coach the Swans.

The Barassi and Smith incidents signalled a change in the game. Professionalism had been around for decades, but now a new sort of professionalism was emerging where a player might dedicate himself full-time to the game, but not necessarily to one club. And clubs too, decided that loyalty ran second to success.

Barassi tasted the ultimate success at Carlton in 1968 but it is his performance in the 1970 Grand Final that is the stuff of legend.

In those days the coach sat on the bench with the trainers and reserve players. But Barassi liked to sit up high so he could see how the game was unfolding tactically. Peter Smith, Norm's son, queued up early on the morning of the grand final, so he could nab a couple of seats in the front row of the Members' Pavilion for himself and Barassi. Who knows what the members sitting around the volatile Barassi had to listen to in that first half. Collingwood, through players like Peter McKenna, dominated to be up by 44 points at the major break.

When the Carlton players came into the rooms at half-time they knew it would be brutal. A few nicked off to the toilets before the coach arrived, trying to avoid the inevitable. Sure

St Kilda defeated the Norm Smith-led Swans in the first semifinal in 1970. It was the Swans' first finals match since the infamous Bloodbath in 1945 and the only one legend Bobby Skilton played in his 237 games.

Alex Jesaulenko (Newspix)

enough as soon as Barassi arrived he upended a table of drinks and then launched into his team. When someone handed him the stats sheet he exploded. "How many handballs do you suppose we've had?" he asked a teenage Robert Walls. The answer was a meagre 16.

Finally Barassi retreated to the blackboard to work out the changes and calm down. When he came back he was a changed man. He refused to give up and told his players that if they let themselves get thrashed they would be shamed for the rest of their lives. It shocked everyone into action. He broke the deficit down into two manageable halves. The Blues needed to recover 22 points, four goals, each quarter. He replaced Bert Thornley with Teddy Hopkins, then, legend has it, he told them to handball at any cost.

They went back out a changed team. Hopkins kicked four goals, Brent Crosswell played a blinder, and in the end Carlton won by 10 points. It was labelled the greatest grand final ever played and to top it off, Alex Jesaulenko took the mark of the century over Graeme 'Jerker' Jenkin.

Legendary Numbers

At the time of writing, there were 18 AFL Hall of Fame Legends. Here are some of the numbers we associate with the Legends.

1 Peter Hudson started his career at Hawthorn wearing the number 26 before changing to number 1. Another number associated with Hudson is 5.64. That was the average number of goals he scored every game—the highest ever in the league, even surpassing John Coleman.

2 AFL Legends John Nicholls (Carlton ruckman) and Ian Stewart (triple Brownlow medallist) both wore the number 2. Stewart wore the number 2 at his second club—Richmond.

3 Three is a champion's number. Ted 'Mr Football' Whitten, Dick 'King Richard' Reynolds, and 'Lethal' Leigh Matthews all wore the number 3.

5 Graham 'Polly' Farmer is an AFL Legend who wore the famous number 5 at Geelong. A few other players who have worn the number 5 but are not yet AFL Legends are: Bernie Quinlan (Fitzroy), James Hird (Essendon), Nathan Buckley (Collingwood) and Gary Ablett (Geelong).

7 AFL Legends that wore the number 7 scored well in the Brownlow medal count. Haydn Bunton wore the number 7 at Fitzroy and won three of the famed Fairest and Best awards. Bill Hutchinson who wore the number 7 in the powerhouse Essendon side of the 1940s and 1950s, won two Brownlows.

10 John Coleman (Essendon), Bob Pratt (South Melbourne) and Barrie Robran (North Adelaide) all wore the number 10. Coleman and Pratt were both fabulous full forwards. Barrie Robran is considered one of the greatest players never to play in the VFL/AFL and he is the only AFL Legend not to have played in that competition. He played his career at North Adelaide where he won three Magarey Medals.

11 Roy 'Up there' Cazaly is remembered by most Swans fans for wearing the number 11, but in his early years at the club he wore the number 1.

14 The number 14 is legendary at South Melbourne. Triple Brownlow medallist and AFL legend, Bobby Skilton wore it. Bill Faul wore it before Bob and Paul Kelly wore it at the Sydney Swans. All three are in the Swans' Team of the Century.

17 Jack Dyer made the number 17 synonymous with Richmond. After his death the club decreed that from then on the Richmond captain would always wear the number 17.

29 Legend has it that Kevin 'Hungry' Bartlett never handballed once in his 403 game career at the Tigers (although there are a few who say they saw him handball once or twice). Bartlett was a brilliant rover and part of five premiership teams.

31 The number 31 will always be associated with Ronald Dale Barassi. He wore it at Melbourne and then at Carlton.

What's in a number?

Collingwood full forward and AFL legend Gordon 'Nuts' Coventry wore several numbers on his back during his career. In those days Collingwood would sometimes assign guernseys alphabetically and the captain wore the number 1. During his long career Nuts wore 3(1934), 5(1921–23, 1937), 6(1924–26, 1936), 7(1927–29,1932), 8(1930–31, 1937), 9(1935), 10(1926), 22(1922) and 29(1920).

Ford

The Times, They Are a Changing

In the 1960s the peace movement, feminism and the sexual revolution had changed the world. As we headed into the 1970s, even conservative Australia loosened up. Gough Whitlam became the first Labor prime minister since 1947. He stopped conscription for the Vietnam War and got rid of the last vestiges of the 'White Australia' policy. His government promoted multiculturalism. His campaign slogan was "It's time", meaning it was time for change. It was time too, for footy clubs to change.

1967 VFL introduces country zoning.

1970 First game played at VFL Park.

1975 Colour television arrives in Australia.

1977 First time VFL grand final is telecast live. It is a draw. North Melbourne win the replay.

1982 South Melbourne move to Sydney and become the Sydney Swans.

Suburban footy

The footy fans of the 1970s had only known a stable and unchanging competition. In the VFL there were 12 teams and all six games were played on Saturday afternoon. If you were a Bombers fan and you were playing at home, you headed off to Windy Hill, Carlton to Princes Park, St Kilda to Moorabbin. Footy was still tribal and while many fans had moved to the outer suburbs, the inner suburb loyalties still existed. You had to have gumption to go and watch your team play away at Victoria Park. The Magpies fans could be passionate to a fault.

Most grounds had a couple of stands but the majority of fans stood to watch the game. Kids propped themselves on eskies or empty beer cans to see over the heads of the other barrackers. The suburban grounds had history and character but they were run-down. Going to the toilet wasn't a particularly pleasant experience.

After the game, the fans would head home and watch the *Game of the Day* replayed on Channel 7. That was it — the most games you could see in one week was two: one live, one on replay.

Television cameras were not as prevalent as they are today and violent incidents would occasionally mar the game. John Greening was Collingwood's youngest player in the 1970 Grand Final. Collingwood lost that day but it didn't change anyone's opinion of Greening — he was going to be a superstar. To prove their belief in him, Collingwood gave the young man coach Bob Rose's old number, 22.

Then in a game between Collingwood and St Kilda at Moorabbin in 1972, Greening was knocked unconscious in an incident behind the play. He was in a semi-coma for several days, and doctors feared at one point for his life. It was one of football's blackest episodes. Greening did eventually return to football but he was never the player he had once been.

The relationship between the VFL and the Melbourne Cricket Club (who manage the MCG) had been stormy since the first ball was bounced. The VFL thought that footy had been subsidising cricket for years, so they decided to build their own stadium out at Mulgrave. At one stage the plan was to build a stadium for a mere 157 000 people (over one and a half times the size of the MCG!).

In 1970 a somewhat smaller stadium, VFL Park, was open for business. Unfortunately the VFL had made some mistakes. The facilities were good but the design meant spectators were a long way from the action and the atmosphere was lost. The wind whipped through and soon enough the new stadium was christened 'Arctic Park' by chilly fans. But the biggest problem was that the only way to get there was by car or bus. There was a lot of talk about a train line, but it was never built. Footy fans walking out of Arctic Park at the end of the game would be stuck by a feeling of panic if they looked down on the acres and acres of car park encircling the ground, and realised they'd forgotten where they'd parked their car.

While the VFL focused on its new ground, the old

traditional suburban grounds were becoming more and more run-down. But despite all of this, many football fans would still describe the days of suburban football in the 1970s as the best of their lives.

Changing of the guard

For years the VFL competition had been dominated by Carlton, Richmond, Essendon, Collingwood and Melbourne. In those days what club you played for depended on what street you grew up in. Each club had a metropolitan area from which players could be selected. The country was a different kettle of fish, and strong clubs like the big five had little problem luring the best country recruits to their club. In 1967 the VFL introduced country zoning to help level the playing field.

In the 1970s Hawthorn and North Melbourne became the powerhouses of the competition, developing a new rivalry. Both had been late additions to the VFL, only admitted in 1925, but the roads they took to success couldn't have been more different.

Ex-player, Allen Aylett took charge of North Melbourne. North had always struggled with membership, and no members meant no money. Without money, success on the footy field was always a little harder. Aylett and his team set about changing North Melbourne into a business. Using money earned from sponsorship deals they bought players from around the country. They also snared the master coach Barassi from the Blues. In 1974 they made

their way to that last Saturday in September, only to be overrun by Richmond. But the next year, Barassi continued his relentless pursuit, shedding players who didn't measure up, and acquiring Malcolm Blight, the South Australian superstar. Once again they made the grand final, this time against the Hawks. The Hawks went in hard but Barassi's men held on. In the end they ran away with it. Fifty years after joining the VFL, the Shinboners had won their first flag and Arden Street, the home of the Kangaroos, partied through the night.

Hawthorn had tasted their first VFL premiership success in 1961, following up with another a decade later. Off-field Hawthorn were one of the most stable clubs in the competition; their administration had undergone very few changes in over 20 years. On-field, coach John Kennedy had built a team style based on strength and endurance. His training methods were the stuff of legend — his players would run drills carrying a sack of wheat on their shoulders. And Hawthorn did extremely well with their country recruits. In the football world, Hawthorn was known as the family club.

Peter Crimmins was a big part of that family; he'd played in their 1971 premiership team and had been made club captain in 1974. But when the Hawks ran out to face the Roos in the 1976 Grand Final, they were led by ruckman Don Scott. Crimmins had cancer and was too ill to play. The Hawks, fielding names like Knights, Matthews and Tuck, were slight favourites. The game was a close encounter for three quarters, Hawthorn's poor kicking keeping North Melbourne in the hunt, but the Hawks finally managed a comfortable 30-point win. After the game, Crimmins's team-mates took the premiership cup to his bedside to share the victory with him. He died three days later. The 1976 premiership will always be known by the Hawthorn faithful as "Crimmo's flag".

At the end of 1976 the VFL presidency was up for grabs, the candidates were Allen Aylett from North Melbourne and Phil Ryan, the Hawthorn president. Aylett got the gig. The VFL was going into business.

Winners and losers

In two games, one year apart, North Melbourne's Malcolm Blight personified the ups and downs of football. In 1976, in a game against Carlton at Princes Park, Blight took a mark between the wing and half forward flank just as the final siren sounded. North Melbourne was trailing by a point but to kick a goal from where he was would take a superhuman effort. To the amazement of everyone, the crowd, his team-mates and the opposition, Blight kicked a massive torpedo that sailed right through the big sticks. The one-eyed Carlton fans were struck dumb and Blight was carried from the field on his team-mates' shoulders. It is still one of the greatest kicks ever filmed.

A year later North Melbourne was playing Hawthorn, trailing by a point. As Blight ran into goal, he was pushed in the back and kicked a point, levelling the scores. The final

siren went but the umpire said Blight could take the kick again if he wanted too. Blight was 20 metres out, directly in front—you bet he wanted to take the kick again. But there was no fairytale ending this time. The ball skewed off his boot, went out of bounds and Hawthorn won.

The Club

In the 1960s, stories about Aussie Rules hit the bookstores, the playhouses and our TV screens. Barry Oakley's *A Salute to the Great McCarthy*, and Alan Hopgood's *And the Big Men Fly* paved the way. Then in early 1977 David Williamson's play, *The Club*, was performed by the Melbourne Theatre Company.

For years Australia had suffered from cultural cringe—where in literature and the arts everything Australian was seen as inferior. Now it was celebrated. And nothing was more Australian than Australian football. Part of this success was due to the continuing ability of Australian football to engage all classes of people. Even the arts community could be found among the barrackers.

David Williamson's play is about power and what it does to men; more specifically it is about the shift of power that was occurring in footy clubs around the country. "*The Club* is about the hangers-on, the end of loyalty, the coming of professionalism, big business and massive transfer fees," wrote Lou Richards. To add to the play's intrigue, theatre-goers who also spent their Saturday afternoons at the footy found some of Williamson's characters all too familiar.

The new wonder coach, who was called Rostoff in the play, was reminiscent of Barassi, and the new recruit had some parallels to a young Brent Crosswell. The club in the play is never specifically mentioned but when the play was made into a film, the players wore black and white.

Collingwood players, including Rene Kink and Ron Wearmouth, make cameo appearances in the film version of The Club.

The club in Williamson's play had only ever had coaches who had been players for the club. In the play, the administrators are trying to break with tradition and woo a new coach from outside. Collingwood coaches too, had always been past players. Then in 1977 they appointed Tom Hafey as coach. It was the first time an outsider had been given the role. Tom Hafey was well qualified; he'd led the Tigers to four premierships in less than a decade. The Magpies team he took over was relatively unchanged from the previous year, but he took them to the grand final — twice in his first year.

Collingwood went into the 1977 Grand Final as favourites; they'd finished on top of the ladder and played well in the finals. North Melbourne, under the direction of Barassi, had had to work hard to win a berth in the biggest game of the season. The game was tight until the third quarter when Collingwood managed to get away yet again to an apparently winning lead of 27 points.

Barassi came out to address North Melbourne. Fashions had changed since 1970. The coach was sporting long hair and a moustache, and the collar on his open-necked shirt looked wide enough that in a stiff breeze Barassi might fly away. His mentor Norm Smith would have been horrified. But while his garb might have changed, the master coach's intensity had not shifted one iota. He harassed and inspired the players, then shuffled the positions around, just as he had seven years before. North came out and played sensationally, pulling to the front. Then with only a minute to go Collingwood's Ross 'Twiggy' Dunne, pulled down a mark and slotted a goal. The final siren sounded. The scores were level, 76 points each. The players fell to the ground exhausted, physically and emotionally.

The hoodoo had hit Collingwood again. They had made the grand final five times since their last premiership in 1958 but not scored a win. In all but one of those encounters, they had been in winnable positions leading into the last quarter. You had to have a strong heart to be a Magpies fan.

The next week in the replay, North Melbourne, perhaps not as weighed down by the expectations of their supporters, managed a comfortable win.

Carn the Blues

Boardroom battles were nothing new to football. They'd

been going on since the time of Tom Wills. But as the game headed into a new era of money men and entrepreneurs, the off-field brawls had stepped up a notch.

George Harris was one of the Blues' most successful presidents, heading up the Blues between the glory years of 1965 and 1974. In 1977 he was back in charge but unusually, he asked to be paid. Presidents of footy clubs had always done the job just for the honour. Harris, like Aylett had with North Melbourne, turned Carlton Football Club into a company and set up a variety of businesses.

The Blues had a good year on the field in 1979. They won the grand final, beating Collingwood again. But behind the scenes things weren't so rosy. Harris was fighting with the rest of the Carlton committee. They didn't like his business ventures. He said they were being disloyal. Carlton's great champion, Alex Jesaulenko, was the captain coach and was loyal to Harris. He said that if Harris left Carlton he would go too. Harris supporters organised a general meeting to resolve the problem, but it backfired. The membership voted out Harris, even though they knew it probably meant their favourite son, the man who'd taken the mark of the century in a navy blue guernsey, would be lost as well. Sure enough Jezza went to St Kilda. They'd always been a tough crowd down at Princes Park.

All this did little to upset the Blues' on-field performances. Two years later the Blues won another flag and followed it up again in 1982.

One of George Harris's most famous failures was the Carlton Bluebirds. Girls in leotards would run onto the field before the game and dance to music, just like American cheerleaders. Geoffrey Edelsten, a mad Carlton supporter, had sponsored the Bluebirds. Later when Edelsten went to Sydney he created the Swanettes. But Australian football fans were simply not interested in this sort of entertainment. Perhaps Harris and Edelsten had forgotten that, unlike American football, nearly half the crowd were women.

The 1982 Grand Final between Richmond and Carlton will always be remembered for the rarest of events—a streaker. Helen D'Amico ran onto the ground during the third quarter wearing only a Carlton scarf. She ran straight at shy Carlton backman Bruce Doull before Wayne 'the Dominator' Johnston dragged her off by her scarf. The Blues went on to win the premiership, their third in four years.

The top end

While football in the VFL was becoming serious business, around the country the game was still being played with enthusiasm and passion by hundreds of suburban and country teams just for the love of it. Each state still had its local league competition and while the VFL thought they were the premier league, you would be hard-pressed to convince the

South Australians, Tasmanians, Western Australians or even the VFA of that.

St Mary's Football Club in Darwin was formed by Ted Egan because there were too many local blackfellas who could not get a game with the other clubs in Darwin. "I knew from seeing them having a kick in the scrub they were good," Egan said.

He was right — since 1952 St Mary's has dominated the Northern Territory competition, winning 25 premierships and developing a number of footballers who went on to play in the VFL. One of the first to come to Melbourne (via South Fremantle) was Maurice Rioli who arrived at Tigerland in 1982. He played in a grand final in his first year winning the Norm Smith Medal. Since then players like Michael Long and the Clarke brothers (Raphael and Xavier) have made their way from St Mary's to the big league.

Football in the Northern Territory is played in the wet season, when the rest of the country is playing cricket, because the ground is too hard in the dry season. Many players say the football played in the Northern Territory is different; the game is unreadable because it is played for the thrill of doing the impossible rather than just kicking a winning score. It makes Northern Territory football spectacular to watch.

Even tough guys cry

Leigh Matthews was built like a mini-tank. He had two

nicknames, Barney Rubble, because he looked just like Fred Flintstone's best mate, and Lethal, because that's how he played. For many, Leigh Matthews is the best they've ever seen.

Matthews started his footy career well. Like Ted Whitten, Matthews's first kick in the VFL was a goal. He went on to become a great ball handler and a prolific goal scorer (Coleman medallist in 1975). He read the game like no one else, but it was his toughness and courage that was second to none. At Windy Hill one day, Matthews tackled a point post; the post split right in half while Matthews just jogged away. In finals footy, Matthews had few rivals. He played in four Hawthorn premiership sides (1971, 1976, 1978 and 1983) and he captained the Hawks for five years.

The last of Lethal's 332 games was in the 1985 Grand Final. It wasn't a fairytale ending with the Bombers annihilating the Hawks. But one of football's most enduring images is the toughest man in football being carried off the field on the shoulders of his mates, tears welling in his eyes.

Despite being a tough player Matthews was not suspended often. In his last year, however, in a game against Geelong, he was involved in a brutal incident that rocked footy and marred an otherwise sensational football career. Matthews broke Neville Bruns's jaw in a clash behind the play, sparking an all-in brawl. The VFL deregistered Matthews for four weeks and police launched an investigation charging Matthews with assault and fining him $1000. This had huge implications for football—a player had been criminally charged for an incident that had occurred on the field. Later, on appeal, the charge was overturned and Matthews was placed on a good behaviour bond, but the precedent had been set.

The 1983 Hawthorn premiership team must hold the record for producing the most coaches of any team. Of the 20 players that day, eight went on to become AFL coaches. Peter Schwab (Hawthorn), Terry Wallace (Bulldogs and Richmond), Rodney Eade (Sydney and the Bulldogs), Gary Ayres (Geelong and Adelaide), Gary Buckenara (Sydney), Peter Knights (Brisbane and Hawthorn), Leigh Matthews (Collingwood and Brisbane) and Ken Judge (Hawthorn and West Coast). Russell Greene, Dermott Brereton and Robert DiPierdomenico have all made careers in the media (where sometimes they think they are the coach).

The VFL didn't want to see the sort of callous acts that had lead to the injuries inflicted on John Greening and Neville Bruns, but they also wanted to keep the physical toughness in the game. But the message was clear—if the game didn't clean up its act then the authorities would do it for them. In fact, in the end, charging of players for on-field incidents did not occur again. Violence on the footy field certainly reduced over the next decade but that had much more to do with television.

Swans fly north

In the old days club champions played footy for a few dollars a week and the fans stood watching the Saturday afternoon game with a pie in one hand and a can in the other. Now footballers were professional and some fans watched from inside the corporate box. Footy was becoming glamorous. And in the 1980s some of the business world's most famous (and later some infamous) businessmen were connected to football.

The VFL wanted to expand and Sydney was the target. Some questioned why. Sydney was the heartland of rugby, lost to Australian football nearly a century before. It was Australia's biggest city but Sydneysiders were not the spectators Melbournians were. They traditionally did not pull the same sized crowds, regardless of the sport. Still the VFL thought that if the code was to go national then Sydney would have to be conquered.

South Melbourne was a club in trouble. They had not played in a grand final since 1945, not won one since 1933, and they only had 1500 members on the books. To save themselves, the committee and the VFL suggested the Swans play all their home games in Sydney on Sundays. The members rebelled. They ousted the committee but found they faced a walkout by the players, most of whom were happy to go to Sydney. To top it off, the new committee had no legal power to determine where their home games should be played, that right belonged to the VFL. In the end the move was unavoidable and the Sydney Swans were officially launched at the Opera House in early 1982.

Imagine the shock this was to the Swans supporters. Footy had had few changes in the decades since the Second World War. Now a whole battalion of fans wondered what to do on wintry Saturday afternoons. Some tried to change their allegiances to other clubs but that was easier said than done. Many just walked away from football altogether.

By 1984 the Sydney experiment was in deep trouble. A white knight appeared in the form of Dr Geoffrey Edelsten. The passionate Carlton supporter was now a flamboyant Sydney doctor. He made a bid to 'buy' the Swans. In America, football clubs are nearly always privately owned — in Australia they are effectively owned by the club's membership, but in this brave new football world the VFL agreed to sell the club for $6.5 million. Edelsten didn't actually have the money onhand himself, so he got another company to put it up.

The next couple of years were exciting times for the Swans. Tom Hafey, one of the era's most successful coaches, was brought on board and Warwick Capper, wearing the tightest shorts in footy, was taking spectacular marks. The crowds increased. Things were looking up. The Swans, for years the lame ducks of the competition, competed in the 1986 and 1987 finals series.

But for one goal

To his adoring fans, Gary Ablett was God.

Gazza grew up in Drouin, in country Victoria, the

youngest of eight kids. All his brothers and sisters were good at sport but Ablett's dad knew his youngest was something special. As a 16-year-old, Ablett was part of Drouin's premiership side. It wouldn't be long before the clubs in the big smoke recognised his talent. As a kid, Ablett's hero was Leigh Matthews and in 1982 he arrived at Matthews's club, Hawthorn. But like a lot of country kids, Ablett didn't enjoy city life. He often missed training to go fishing or rabbiting. In the end he only managed half a dozen games with the Hawks before he was back in the country leagues. Geelong knew the kid had talent and chased him. For Ablett, Geelong offered the best of both worlds, league football in a country town environment. They convinced him to head down the coast and pull on Geelong's famous hoops. Ablett would still occasionally miss training to go fishing but Geelong put up with it as long as he followed up on the weekend with sensational football.

In the 1980s the VFL hit a crisis. The unbelievable was happening—attendances were falling. In the early 1960s the average attendance during a home and away round was about 7 per cent of the population of Melbourne, by the mid 1980s it was down to only 4.6 per cent. The drop in attendances seemed to mirror a rise in the price of admission. As a percentage of the average person's weekly earnings, the price of an admission ticket had doubled. Gary Ablett's skills were so astonishing that thousands of spectators who didn't barrack for Geelong would roll up to games just to watch Ablett play. For the VFL Ablett was a godsend. He helped revitalise the game.

People argue endlessly about who was the greatest player to ever pull on the footy boots — Matthews or Ablett. Matthews was tough, if not spectacular. He loved the extra pressure of finals football. The team he played for became a winning team. Ablett took sensational marks and kicked freakish goals. But interestingly two of his greatest games were in losing teams.

The 1989 Grand Final was one of the toughest and most exciting of all time. Dermott Brereton was thumped in the first few minutes but refused to leave the field. Before the first break Platten was flattened and in the second quarter Robert DiPierdomenico had his ribs broken and a lung punctured. Despite this, Hawthorn led most of the day by more than a handy lead. But Geelong had God on their side. He kicked an amazing nine goals bringing the Cats back within a measly six points — one goal — but that was as

After Gary Ablett retired from football, a young woman in his company died after taking drugs. Controversially this incident has excluded him from being included in the AFL's Hall of Fame, despite Geelong nominating him each year.

close as they would get. Ablett won the Norm Smith, but missed out on a premiership medal.

A few years later Geelong faced up to Essendon at the MCG. Ablett, his thinning mullet blowing in the breeze, kicked a magnificent 14.7. Still his team lost. He may well have been the most sensational player of all time, but even his superhuman efforts couldn't seem to get his team over the line.

The Clubs

Adelaide
The Crows

Formed: 1990

First year played in AFL: 1991

Premierships: 1997, 1998

Malcolm Blight, originally a South Australian, coached the Crows to their first flag.

Brisbane
Lions

Formed: 1996 (Fitzroy and the Brisbane Bears merged to create the Brisbane Lions. Fitzroy was formed in 1883, the Brisbane Bears in 1986.)

First year played in VFL/AFL: Brisbane Lions 1997, Fitzroy 1897, Brisbane Bears 1987.

Premierships: Fitzroy—1898, 1899, 1904, 1905, 1913, 1916, 1922, 1944. Brisbane Lions—2001, 2002, 2003.

Before they were the Lions, Fitzroy were known as the Maroons and the Gorillas

Carlton
The Blues

Formed: 1864

First year played in VFL: 1897

Premierships: 1906, 1907, 1908, 1914, 1915, 1938, 1945, 1947, 1968, 1970, 1972, 1979, 1981, 1982, 1987, 1995

Carlton was known as the Butchers for a short time in the early days. Their motto, Mens Sano Incorpora Sano, means A Healthy Mind in a Healthy Body.

Collingwood
The Magpies

Formed: 1892
First year played in VFL: 1897
Premierships: 1902, 1903, 1910, 1917, 1919, 1927, 1928, 1929, 1930, 1935, 1936, 1953, 1958, 1990
Collingwood's motto Floreat Pica means May the Magpie Prosper.

Essendon
Bombers

Formed: 1873
First year played in VFL: 1897
Premierships: 1897, 1901, 1911, 1912, 1923, 1924, 1942, 1946, 1949, 1950, 1962, 1965, 1984, 1985, 1993, 2000
Back in the 1800s Essendon were known as the Same Olds but later their closeness to the airport earned them the title Bombers.

Fremantle
Dockers

Formed: 1994
First year played AFL: 1995
Premierships: None
East and South Fremantle always had a fierce rivalry in the WAFL.

Geelong
The Cats

Formed: 1859

First year played in VFL: 1897

Premierships: 1925, 1931, 1937, 1951, 1952, 1963

Geelong was known as the Pivotonians in their early days.

Hawthorn
The Hawks

Formed: 1902

First year played in VFL: 1925

Premierships: 1961, 1971, 1976, 1978, 1983, 1986, 1988, 1989, 1991

Hawthorn was known as the Mayblooms before Roy Cazaly changed it to Hawks.

Kangaroos

Formed: 1869

First year played in VFL: 1925

Premierships: 1975, 1977, 1996, 1999

The Kangaroos started life as Hotham, then a couple of years later became North Melbourne before a recent change to the Kangaroos. In the early days they had the unofficial nickname of Shinboners.

Melbourne
Demons

Formed: 1858

First year played in VFL: 1897

Premierships: 1900, 1926, 1939, 1940, 1941, 1948, 1955, 1956, 1957, 1959, 1960, 1964

Melbourne, the oldest club, has had heaps of nicknames including, Invincible Whites, Fuchsias and Red Legs.

Port Adelaide
Power

Formed: 1870 (Port Adelaide Magpies)

First year played AFL: 1997

Premierships: 2004

The Port Adelaide Magpies still compete in the SANFL and have 36 SANFL premierships.

Richmond
The Tigers

Formed: 1885

First year played in VFL: 1908

Premierships: 1920, 1921, 1932, 1934, 1943, 1967, 1969, 1973, 1974, 1980

Various 'Richmond' football clubs existed before 1885, but the current club was formed in 1885. For a short time they were known as the Wasps.

St Kilda
The Saints

Formed: 1873

First year played in VFL: 1897

Premierships: 1966

South Yarra had been disbanded the year before St Kilda formed. Many South Yarra players joined the new club.

Sydney
The Swans

Formed: 1874

First year played in VFL: 1897

Premierships: 1909, 1918, 1933

South Melbourne was known as the Blood-stained Angels before the 1930s. South Melbourne moved to Sydney in 1982 and became the Sydney Swans.

West Coast
Eagles

Formed: 1986

First year played in AFL: 1987

Premierships: 1992, 1994

Mick Malthouse was coach for West Coast's two flags.

Western Bulldogs

Formed: 1883

First year played in VFL: 1925

Premierships: 1954

Footscray changed their name to the Western Bulldogs in 1997. Footscray were once known as the Tricolours.

Nationalisation or Bust

In the 1980s, the motto was "greed is good". Entrepreneurs like Christopher Skase and Alan Bond became household names. They spent big and they spent extravagantly. They even dabbled in football clubs. But the inevitable stock market crash came and the entrepreneurs' paper castles were blown away. Despite the crash, the foundations of a new game built around big business had been laid. The average barracker had to become familiar with a few new footy terms: rationalisation, equalisation and nationalisation.

1986 VFL moves to the National Player Draft.

1987 West Coast Eagles and Brisbane Bears play their first games in the VFL.

Stock market crash.

1990 VFL change their name to the Australian Football League (AFL).

1991 Adelaide play their first game in the AFL.

1994 *The Footy Show* featuring Eddie McGuire and Sam Newman first goes to air.

1995 Fremantle play their first game in the AFL.

VFA change their name to the VFL.

1996 Fitzroy play their last League match.

1997 Brisbane Bears merge with Fitzroy and become the Brisbane Lions.

Port Adelaide play their first game in the AFL.

Equalisation

While some clubs found themselves competing in the finals year after year, others, like Footscray, Fitzroy and St Kilda had always struggled, both on and off the field. It takes a lot of dedication to turn up week after week to watch your team play, knowing that you will more than likely walk away losers. Doggie, Lions and Saints fans had shown amazing dedication, but they couldn't draw new fans, and the clubs struggled for members.

In 1985 the League wrote a policy of equalisation to ensure success was spread around and not hogged by the lucky few. The zoning system had only been marginally successful in creating a level playing field. Interstate players could still be 'bought' and some country areas simply produced stronger recruits.

The League's policy of equalisation had a couple of cornerstones. Firstly, all money raised by the League, by selling the TV rights for example, would be split evenly among the clubs. Secondly, the total amount of money a club could pay its players was capped, so rich clubs could not 'buy' premierships. And lastly, zoning was replaced by the draft. In the draft all prospective players were put into a pool. The clubs that had finished on the bottom of the ladder were given first pick of the best young talent in the country.

It took a few years for the clubs to really understand the drafting system and to make it work to their advantage but over the years it has become one of the most important

elements of League football. But the loss of zoning had an effect on country football. In the old days clubs 'owned' a country area and it was in their interests to develop the game in those towns. Often those towns then also became supporter strongholds for the club, as their young men headed off to the big city to play League. The national draft, on the other hand, meant a 17-year-old who'd never been out of his state might have to move from country Western Australia to Brisbane, leaving all his family and friends behind.

Alistair Lynch was picked up in the first draft of 1986. When he played in the 2004 Grand Final he was the last of the players drafted that year to still be playing. Lynch walked away from the game with three premiership medallions won with the Brisbane Lions.

Girls in the dressing room

Corrie Perkin started covering football for *The Age* in the early 1980s. It was an absolutely radical notion at the time for a woman to be covering football, but the paper was supportive. Not so the footy clubs. One of the most important aspects for a reporter is being able to interview the players in the change rooms after the game. In her first match, Corrie was kicked out of the Hawthorn rooms by captain Leigh

Matthews, even after her male colleagues, some from the opposition newspaper, stood up for her. After a few letters between the paper and the club, the issue was resolved.

Caroline Wilson (Caro to everyone in football) grew up a passionate Richmond supporter. She had no choice — her dad was president of the club from 1974 to 1985. Ironically when Caroline started out as a journalist for the *Herald* newspaper, the only club that still banned female reporters from the change rooms was Richmond.

Nationalisation

For over 60 years (with the exception of the war years) the same 12 teams had competed in the VFL. South Melbourne had relocated but it still carried the traditions of a century-old club. In 1987 the VFL agreed to let two new teams join — one from Brisbane and one from Western Australia. It was the start of an upheaval that would shake football for the next decade. Nationalisation of the competition was well and truly on the agenda.

The clubs voted unanimously for a new team from Brisbane, but only the minimum two-thirds voted for the inclusion of a Western Australian team. No doubt the vote was led by self-interest. Brisbane was unlikely to present a competitive threat for the premiership. Western Australia, on the other hand, had a pool of exceptional talent to choose from and had potential to be competitive from day one. But joining the VFL didn't come cheap and most clubs wanted their share of the hefty licence fee they

would charge the Western Australians.

The Brisbane licence was won by a syndicate headed by actor Paul Cronin (he played Dave in *The Sullivans*). When it came to the crunch, however, the Cronin syndicate didn't actually have all the money. That's when entrepreneur Christopher Skase agreed to make up the balance and the Brisbane Bears were born. Brisbane did okay in its first couple of years but struggled after that and quickly became known as the 'bad news Bears'. They had little access to players and they were trying to develop a supporter base in a town that loved rugby league. The other clubs were happy to pocket their part of the licence fee but were not prepared to make any other concessions. The Western Australian licence was bought by the WAFL who hoped to stop the flow of star players to Victoria. They had the talent and a footy-mad public to play for, and just as the other VFL clubs had feared, the West Coast Eagles were competitive from the beginning.

The only problem was that most of the clubs in the WAFL relied on the player transfer fees they got when a player moved to Victoria to stay afloat. If players stayed within the state, they wouldn't get that money. To raise money the WAFL sub-licensed the club to another company. The West Coast Eagles now had to make enough money to pay the AFL and WAFL their cuts as well as run a profit. There were too many hands in the cookie jar and not enough to go around. Not even a successful team could make that much.

Then the stock market crashed, sending the world into another economic depression and the effects rippled across the football world. The company behind the Swans went under and sold the club for $10 back to the VFL who sold it on to another group for over $4.5 million. Skase's business eventually collapsed and the licence for the Bears also changed hands. Skase headed off to Spain, but that's another story.

Also during those heady days a number of clubs had listed themselves on the stock market. The idea was to raise money, but it also gave shareholders extraordinary voting powers compared to the average member. Club power brokers bought up shares and used their votes to get approval for things that the majority of members didn't want. St Kilda moved from Moorabbin to Waverley and Collingwood and Essendon to the MCG, against the wishes of the majority of members. But being listed on the stock market could backfire too. Bob Ansett listed North Melbourne on the stock market to raise some capital but when the market crashed it became clear that a company called Tricontinental was the majority shareholder. Rumours spread that the vultures were circling and Carlton were going to buy North Melbourne from Tricontinental to get the best of their players. Luckily for North Melbourne, legal reasons prevented this.

The new owners of the Bears and the Swans still couldn't make ends meet and both clubs were eventually returned to the traditional membership structure. The experiment

with the American private ownership model had failed, much like the Bluebirds had bombed a few years before. Experienced businessmen had been fooled into thinking you could make your fortune in football.

Up yours Oakley

Three non-Victorian clubs were not enough to realise the VFL's dream of nationalisation, but they needed some of the existing clubs to merge before they could expand further. In 1989 they thought their wishes had been answered.

"People from Brighton Grammar are making decisions about the western suburbs. It's just not on. The silvertails have absconded with our football club in the middle of the night."
Les Twentyman, a community worker in the western suburbs.

Footscray and Fitzroy were struggling financially and merging seemed the only way out. But the VFL had misjudged the mood in the suburbs. Irate fans were not happy with the changes to the competition. What did they care for national competitions and new clubs from interstate? The average Bulldogs' fan didn't have a lot of spare cash, but they had passion. Ross Oakley, head of the VFL at the time, was targeted for attack. "Up Yours Oakley" bumper stickers started appearing around

Footscray. The fans rallied, raising funds by doorknocking and roadside collection. Finally a sponsorship deal with ICI, which had a large factory in the western suburbs, saved the club from a merger.

At the end of 1989 the VFL symbolically changed their name to the Australian Football League. Six years later the VFA was restructured and renamed the VFL, effectively becoming a feeder competition to the AFL. In the first 50 years of footy the fiercest rivalry in Melbourne had not been between Collingwood and Carlton but the VFL and the VFA. Now that rivalry had ended in a whimper.

The first grand final in the new AFL was not won by one of the new interstate clubs but by one of the competition's traditional powerhouses. In 1990 Collingwood buried 32 years of Collywobble jokes. Collingwood had appeared in nine grand finals (if you count both appearances in 1977) since their last win in 1958, only to fail at the last hurdle every time. To make matters worse many of those grand finals were lost by slender margins or after they had been in seemingly winnable positions. To describe this repeated failure, Collingwood champion Lou Richards had coined the term the Collywobbles. But 1990 ensured that was all water under the bridge.

The Pies weren't in scintillating form leading into the finals. Centreman Darren Millane had to play with a busted thumb that he got re-plastered after each game, and Collingwood only managed a draw with West Coast in the first Qualifying Final. But after that near miss they

recovered well, and with Leigh Matthews at the helm, they went into the grand final favourites At quarter-time, with the scores separated by just three points, a brawl erupted and Collingwood's Gavin Brown was knocked unconscious. But this was the Pies' day and, unlike the grand finals of the past, their concentration didn't break. They went on to win comfortably, beating Essendon, 89 to 41. The Magpie army seemed relieved rather than ecstatic. As one unnamed fan declared, "Now we can get on with the rest of our lives."

Just over a year after Darren Millane had drunk from the premiership cup, he was killed in a horrific car accident. Just as Carlton had done when George Coulthard died over 100 years before, all of Collingwood went into mourning.

Go west

The AFL decided they didn't need a merger to add another team. The SANFL is a proud competition—they never accepted that the Victorian competition was superior. They decided very early on that if one of their teams was to join the AFL, then they wouldn't be paying a licence fee for the privilege. Port Adelaide, the strongest club in the SANFL, broke ranks and started talks with the AFL, causing all sorts of problems. Other clubs in the SANFL started legal action to stop the discussions and back in Victoria, Collingwood were worried that Port Adelaide would keep their black and white guernseys and Magpie emblem. With their unity broken the SANFL gave in and agreed to pay the licence fee. Like the WAFL they decided to create a new club, and the Adelaide Crows became part of the AFL fixture in 1991. Port Adelaide's attempts to jump the gun kept them out of the AFL for a few years yet.

The end of Adelaide's first year coincided with the first appearance of one of the new teams in a grand final. West Coast faced Hawthorn on the last Saturday in September, not at the home of football, the MCG, but at Waverley (VFL) Park. The MCG was out of action as the new Great Southern Stand was being built. The consistent Eagles were slightly favoured to win the flag, although their opponents were the highly talented Hawks. But experience won over consistency and the Hawks added another premiership to the trophy cabinet.

In the 1993 pre-season, Nigel Smart from Adelaide walked on hot coals in a test of mind over matter. Unfortunately Nigel's mind didn't prevail and he suffered bad burns to both his feet.

After the game, Michael Tuck, with an amazing 426 VFL/AFL games to his credit,

retired. It was also the end of an extraordinary run for Hawthorn. They had played in every grand final from 1983 to 1991, with the exception of 1990, and had won five flags. They, like Jock McHale's Collingwood side of the 1920s, and Norm Smith's Melbourne side of the 1950s, had dominated an era. But as the Hawks slid out of contention in the years to follow, West Coast's fortunes were on the rise. They were back the next year for their first flag — won this time on the sacred turf of the MCG. It was the first time the AFL Premiership Cup was to be taken out of Victoria, but it was hardly going to be the last time.

On radio station 3XY a young television reporter called his first grand final in 1990. That young reporter was Eddie McGuire and he went on to become president of Collingwood and host of the popular Footy Show.

Professionalism

While the rest of the competition was worrying about going national, Ron Barassi, always the innovator, was thinking international. In the 1980s Barassi convinced Melbourne to offer opportunities to Gaelic footballers. Melbourne's offer was written up in the local Irish papers as a fabulous opportunity for young men to travel to balmy Australia and make a living as a footballer. A few played senior football, but it was Jim Stynes who stood out. In 1991 Stynes won the Brownlow Medal and by the time his career was over he'd set a new record of 244 consecutive league matches.

Football had been professional since 1911. Over the years, just what that meant in terms of income for players had changed. From the 1930s to the 1950s a player's income was limited by the Coulter Law which meant he could get around two thirds of the minimum weekly wage for a game, equivalent of about $300 a game today. In the 1970s a player would earn around 75 per cent of the average weekly earnings for a game, about $750 a game in today's money. By 1993 more and more players were fully professional; football was their only job. They became concerned about their conditions, being looked after when they were injured and getting a fair slice of the money the game was generating. That year the AFL Players Association, headed up by Carlton ruckman Justin Madden, was able to negotiate a collective agreement with the AFL over players pay and conditions.

By 2003 the minimum contract was $43 000 a year. A champion player could be on about $300 000 or $400 000 a year, and with sponsorship deals it could be a lot more.

Nicky's black skin

If you'd checked out the kids milling around the fence line at any St Kilda game in the early 1990s, you'd notice that most wore the number 7 on their backs. St Kilda boasted

the hulking Tony Lockett at full forward, but for the kids Nicky Winmar, with his flying leaps and miraculous sprints down the wing, was king. 1993 was Nicky's seventh season with the Saints and it was also the International Year of Indigenous People. In April the Saints headed off to the worst of the suburban football grounds, Victoria Park, to face the Pies. Lockett was suspended but Nicky and fellow Aboriginal player Gilbert McAdam humiliated Collingwood all over the ground. The more they pounded the Pies the more the infamous Collingwood cheersquad hurled racial abuse at the two. After St Kilda won the game Nicky turned to the Magpie army, lifted his guernsey and pointed to his black skin. His message—I'm black and I'm proud.

The International Year of Indigenous People, 1993, ended on a fitting note when Gavin Wanganeen won the Brownlow Medal, and Michael Long had the Norm Smith Medal presented to him by his hero, Maurice Rioli. All three are Aboriginal.

Nicky's stand became one of the defining moments in football. Racial abuse, not just from fans but from other players, and discrimination by clubs, had plagued football since the first Aboriginal players had picked up a football.

Collingwood president Allan McAlister showed that ignorance was not confined to the cheersquad when he later said, "As long as they [Aborigines] conduct themselves like white people... everyone will admire and respect them." Now the time had come when enough was enough.

The AFL attempted to introduce a code of conduct, but it was still not in place a couple of years later when Aboriginal player Michael Long was racially abused by Collingwood ruckman Damian Monkhorst. Long complained and the AFL tried to smooth things over, but Long was far from happy with the outcome—Monkhorst had not actually apologised in the conciliation session. The resulting publicity and several more racial vilification complaints (not all involving Aborigines) put a bomb under the AFL and eventually a racial vilification policy was put in place.

In fact the AFL had achieved what federal parliament could not—Labor could not get a similar policy through the Senate. The racial vilification policy was one of the AFL's greatest achievements in recent times. In the first 80 years of League football there had been only about 20 players with Aboriginal heritage. Throughout the 1990s this percentage increased dramatically and today the percentage of Aborigines playing Australian football is higher than the percentage of the total population that is Aboriginal.

Rationalisation

For the 1995 season the AFL approved a licence for a

second Western Australian team. Fremantle was officially a new team, but it was linked to a rich history of football. East and South Fremantle are traditional rivals who have been battling it out since the start of the 20th century. The Fremantle dockyards bred hard men and tough footballers. The new club became known as the Dockers.

The AFL had agreed to give Port Adelaide a licence but only as part of a 16-club competition. That meant another club had to fold or merge and Fitzroy were the likely contenders. For a short while it looked like the ailing Lions might merge with North Melbourne but the other clubs, always looking after their own interests, were not having that. The Kangaroos had just won the flag and merging with Fitzroy would only bolster their already impressive playing list. The only other option was a merge with the bad news Bears.

Fitzroy were in all sorts of financial trouble. They had been bailed out in the past with a loan from the little island nation Nauru, but now Nauru wanted their money back and Fitzroy didn't have it. A merger with Brisbane would get Nauru some of their money. The accountant employed by Nauru agreed, and that was that. In one of the saddest days in football, 113 years of history were gone on the say of an accountant and the members couldn't do a thing about it. Fitzroy's situation was different to South Melbourne's years before. The Swans had picked themselves up lock, stock and barrel and moved to Sydney but the club itself continued. Fitzroy were merging with another club, their identity was being muddied.

Fitzroy's last game was to be played in Perth against the League's newest recruits, Fremantle, so for many local fans their last opportunity to see their team play was in Round 21 in 1996 when Fitzroy faced Richmond at the MCG. The Tigers belted the Lions but it didn't seem to matter to the supporters. When it was all over, they ran onto the field, following the players back into the change rooms and refusing to leave. They sang the song like they had never sung it before and would never sing it again. "We are the boys of old Fitzroy, We wear the colours maroon and blue, We will always fight for victory, We will always see it through, Win or lose, we do or die, In defeat we always try, Fitzroy, Fitzroy, The club we hold so dear, Premiers we'll be this year."

But they wouldn't be premiers that year or the next. The new Brisbane would be known as the Lions and wear a modified Fitzroy guernsey, but for many diehard fans it simply wasn't the same. A lot of supporters walked away from the MCG that day vowing never to watch another football game again. It was a reminder that fans don't support the AFL, they may love the game and even individual players, but for many their fanatic loyalty is all about the club.

Port Adelaide finally got their licence to play in the AFL but they had to change their colours and their mascot. Teal blue was added to the guernsey to differentiate it from Collingwood's, and they became the Power. Fittingly they

played their first match in the AFL against the Pies at the MCG. They lost.

While the AFL had wanted at least one merger — there wasn't any reason others couldn't follow. Financially strapped Melbourne and Hawthorn looked like likely contenders in 1996. Those in favour of the merger pointed out the two clubs had similar supporter bases — middle to upper class. But former ruckman for the Hawks, Don Scott, was against the merger and formed Operation Payback to raise the money to cover Hawthorn's debts.

Melbourne's opposition to the merger came later, in the form of Demon Alternative. They recruited mining magnate Joseph Gutnick, who pledged $3 million to the Demons. Gutnick is also an ultra-orthodox Jew. He observes the Sabbath (or Shabbat in Hebrew), a day of rest and spiritual enrichment, on Saturday. There are lots of things, like working or driving a car, that are restricted on the Sabbath. When Melbourne played on Saturday, Gutnick wasn't able to go and watch his team — and that included when the team made the grand final in 2000. Melbourne's members voted narrowly for the merger, Hawthorn against. There was no merger.

Most, Tallest, Shortest

Most games for the VFL/AFL

Michael Tuck (Hawthorn)—426 games.

Most games for the WAFL

Mel Whinnen (West Perth)—371 games.

Most games for the SANFL

Peter Carey (Glenelg)—448 games.

Most games at senior level (VFL/AFL, SANFL, State and International)

Craig Bradley—501 games, Port Adelaide (98), Carlton (375), South Australia (19) and International (9).

Tall and short

At 211 cm (6 foot 11 inches) Aaron Sandilands (Fremantle) is, at the time of writing, the tallest player to play AFL. James 'Nipper' Bradford played for Collingwood and North Melbourne in the 1940s; he was only 155 cm (5 foot 1 inch) tall.

1999
TO NOW

Going Forward

The expansion of the competition throughout the country had been painful. Many fans were upset at losing traditional suburban football. The clubs were changing and the old grounds were gone. There was animosity towards what people saw as corporate football, but corporate speak was here to stay. Club presidents talked about going forward instead of climbing the ladder, coaches talked about setting goals instead of kicking them. Still the AFL could only be ecstatic with the national competition as the non-Victorian clubs did well, and after the doldrums of the 1980s, attendances rose again. And, as always, there were plenty of controversies to fill the newspapers.

2000 First game played at the new stadium at Docklands.

2002 A group consisting of Channels 10, 9 and Foxtel win the rights to telecast football ending a decades-old relationship between Channel 7 and the League.

Carlton are found guilty of breaching the salary cap for a second time and are fined $1 million and excluded from the draft.

2003 Brisbane win their third premiership in succession.

2005 Last game played at Optus Oval (Princes Park) — the end of suburban football in metropolitan Melbourne.

Final hurrah

When Victoria faced South Australia in the 1995 State of Origin match, Ted Whitten was gravely ill, suffering from cancer. Before the game Ted went down into the Victorian changerooms to chat to the players. Danny Frawley looked after Ted, whispering in Ted's ear the name of each player who came over. The cancer had blinded Ted, but he didn't want the players to know. The Big V was well represented on the forward line that day, with Gary Ablett playing alongside Tony Lockett. When Lockett asked Ted how he was going Ted said, "Don't worry about me, are you alright? You're the one who's gotta go out and kick some goals."

Just before the first bounce a car drove Ted around the MCG one last time. The song "Hero" played over the loud speakers. "I sat in the car with him and gave him my coat because he was shivering, and he was getting wound up, getting the old 'stick it up 'em' going," said Frawley. Sitting next to his dad was Ted Whitten Jnr. He held up his old man and described the scene as the car drove around. When the car got to Ted's old foe and good mate, South Australian Neil Kerley, the two men hugged. In the stands fans and old mates wept as they said goodbye.

Ted died soon after and Footscray renamed their old home ground Whitten Oval. It was one ground name change that everyone agreed with.

'The people's ground'—the MCG—is staffed by a group of long-serving employees known affectionately as the 'redcoats'. Many redcoats can recall Barry Breen's point

and Jezza's mark. They can talk about the great cricket matches and the first day they flicked the switch to turn on the new light towers. But many of the men and women who were there that day will tell you that the raw emotion in crowd, when Ted said his final goodbyes, was unsurpassed and the most memorable. It was proof that footy means more to people than just what happens during the game.

After Ted died, so did State of Origin football. The last game was played in 1999. In the past State of Origin had been a way for the fans to see the best talent in the country. The argument was that now the competition was national, they saw it every week.

"We stuck it up 'em; we stuck it up 'em. Victoooriaaa. Victoooriaaa." Ted Whitten after Victoria beat South Australia in Adelaide.

There's only one Tony Lockett

That day when Tony 'Plugger' Lockett shared the forward line with 'God' (Gary Ablett) many thought he was the better player of the two. Yet when Plugger had arrived at Moorabbin back in 1983 he thought he was a ruckman. Four years later he'd won a Brownlow and kicked 117 goals, well and truly claiming full forward as his own.

In 1995, with an astonishing 898 goals to his

credit, Plugger packed up his old Adidas training bag and left the Saints for the Sydney Swans. Surprisingly, the move to Sydney seemed to suit the guy from Ballarat. Life in the Rugby League city was a little simpler for someone who didn't like the limelight. And Sydney loved Plugger. It was only a year later that he kicked a point after the siren in the preliminary final against Essendon to give the Swans their first shot at a flag since 1945. The Sydney supporters, apparently unaware of modern football protocols, surged onto the field in mass hysteria. Their unrestrained joy only lasted a week. The Swans came up against a very determined Kangaroos outfit in the final game of the season and they didn't have what it took to break a 63-year drought.

"The Grand Old Duke of York he had ten thousand men. He put them all on Tony Lockett and he still kicked ten."

Guru Bob from radio's "Coodabeen Champions".

In fact Plugger never acquired a premiership medallion, but in June 1999 he created a piece of history at the Sydney Cricket Ground when his good mate Paul Kelly chipped the ball to him and he went back and slotted it through the big sticks. Against the Pies, in front of more than 40 000 fans, Tony had just kicked his 1300th goal, breaking Gordon 'Nuts' Coventry's longstanding record.

So it was that one of the most enduring records in Australian football was broken at a ground famous for another game, in a city that loved another code of football. For a while the Rugby League city was won over to Aussie Rules and the airwaves were saturated with a new song, "There's only one Tony Lockett".

The national competition was here to stay. West Coast had won two flags, as had Adelaide. Nearly as many Sydneysiders watched the Swans lose to the Kangaroos in 1996 as had watched the Rugby League final. But without doubt the dominance of Brisbane in the new millennium rankled the Victorians the most. After their first flag against the Bombers, many Victorians were happy to see a resurrected Fitzroy do well, but that goodwill didn't last. In an effort to promote the game in the non-traditional Australian football states, the AFL had allocated slightly higher salary caps to Brisbane and Sydney. The Victorian clubs saw this as an unfair advantage. Of course nothing is that simple — despite this supposed advantage, Sydney has not tasted ultimate success and on the other side of the ledger the perennially cash-strapped Kangaroos had done well over the last decade. In an effort to break down the barriers between the states it was decreed that Melbournians should stop referring to clubs from other states as "interstate clubs" and call them non-Victorian clubs. Which was fair enough — Collingwood and Carlton are interstate clubs if you live in Perth.

Grounds for the theatregoers

A footy ground is the vessel that holds a million memories. Diehard fans will talk animatedly about where they were sitting and what they saw the day Blighty kicked his spearing torpedo or when Lethal broke the point post. But the suburban grounds could not keep pace. The seats were often broken, the pies were cold and the smell of stale pee wafted out of the toilet block. It could be pretty hard going if you were supporting the away team at one of the rougher home grounds. And many suburban grounds turned into muddy bogs when the rain came. The fans were changing — they wanted to sit in a seat, have a latte at half-time and catch the train home. Footy players were changing too — they wouldn't put up with the shoddy conditions of the past anymore. Suburban footy grounds were becoming extinct.

> *"They just surrounded us and pelted us with cigarette butts and beer cans. We approached a policeman who said he couldn't do anything about it and he added he was a Collingwood supporter anyway."*
>
> West Coast cheersquad member at Victoria Park.

In the first round of the first year in the new millennium, Essendon faced up to Port Adelaide at the game's newest stadium in Melbourne's

Docklands. This was the stadium for the future, designed for the new footy fan, labelled "theatregoers". Fans were closer to the action and there was a retractable roof that could be closed if the heavens opened up. The new stadium had its teething problems (it is difficult to grow grass in the shade) but soon drew large crowds. In a competitive environment even the MCG needed a facelift and in 2002 construction commenced on the new Northern Stand. When Carlton announced they would play their last game at Optus Oval (Princes Park) in 2005, it was the end of suburban football in metropolitan Melbourne. Geelong's Skilled Stadium (Kardinia Park) becoming the last truly home ground in Victoria.

Image management

A good whack of the new money in football had come from television. It was a double-edged sword. The AFL needed the media to promote the game but the media wouldn't simply report stories that made the game look good. In fact some cynics would say it was the sordid stories that were of most interest. Throughout the 1990s and into the 2000s various controversies kept the AFL on their toes.

In 1997, Tiger Justin Charles, tested positive to a performance-enhancing drug. He admitted he had injected himself with anabolic steroids to overcome injuries and was suspended for 16 games. Performance-enhancing drugs have not been the headline stealer in AFL as they have been in other sports. In footy the hot topic has been recreational drugs (drugs that are illegal but do not have a positive effect on the players' athletic performance). In 2004 two Carlton players arrived at training obviously under the influence of the drug ecstasy. Carlton had the two players tested, sacked one and suspended the other. This incident opened a can of worms. What right did the AFL or the clubs have to test players for recreational drugs, particularly out of season? However, these drugs are illegal. Why should players think they have a right to privacy? But drug use is just one of the issues the AFL is tackling.

With nationalisation, the administrators had to sell the game to spectators who hadn't grown up with footy in their blood, but just as the game was becoming successful interstate they had a more local audience they had to convince.

Imagine the parents of a 10-year-old watching the 1989 Grand Final. They see Brereton hit the deck and the colossal Dipper given a few broken ribs to go on with. When their son declares he wants to play in the little league, no doubt they find good reasons to turn him to basketball or soccer. Television changed the way we see football. Mostly it was good—more games, different angles, access to every statistic you could ever want to know, but it also exposed footy's occasional brutality. Footy is a tough contact sport but sometimes players, even champion players, cross the line from aggression to violence. With television we see it all, over and over again, on replay. Any player from the 1960s and 1970s will tell you the game's a lot cleaner now than it was back in their day. Still one of the greatest

challenges facing the AFL is to create a game that parents are happy for their kids to play and yet maintain the toughness that makes the game such a fabulous spectacle.

"I can't understand why Matthew Lloyd would do that. There are more cameras pointed at Friday night football than you'd find in a Tokyo airport departure lounge."
Dennis Cometti after Bomber Matthew Lloyd was involved in an on-field indiscretion.

But at least most kids still dream of one day doing a 'Barry Breen' and scoring the winning point in the final minutes of a grand final. Not many grow up wanting to bounce the ball to start the game. In Australian football there are three field umpires, two boundary umpires and two goal umpires in a game. The umpire's job is a difficult one—the rules are highly interpretive, the umpire cannot send a player off the field during the game like in soccer, they have to be very fit and be able to bounce the ball true. And they have to do all of this while being abused by the fans. Historically Australians have not respected authority and the umpires represent authority. In an attempt to lure umpires to the junior ranks the AFL is trying to change a century of attitudes. How they go about that is the difficult question.

The Bombers have been blessed with a long

history of gentlemanly champions, from Dick Reynolds and John Coleman to the latest incarnation, James Hird. Famously, Hird, a skinny kid from Canberra, was taken in the 1990 draft with pick 79. It was the bargain of the century. Like his predecessors, Hird is highly skilled and courageous to his own detriment. He played in the 1993 baby Bombers premiership side and won a Brownlow. He battled through the 1997 and 1998 seasons with a crippling foot injury but thought that was all behind him when the 1999 season started. But only two rounds in it reappeared, and James was left sitting on the boundary crying with frustration. As no doubt did all the Bomber fans, who must have thought the curse of John Coleman had come to claim their captain. But Hird showed extraordinary fortitude, continued his rehabilitation and at the end of the next year he was standing upon the dais holding the premiership cup aloft. He is quite simply one of the greatest players of his generation.

Hird's good looks and obvious intelligence also made him the perfect poster-boy for the AFL and a natural for television. Then in 2004, on *The Footy Show*, he described umpire Scott McLaren's skills as "disgraceful". The fallout was huge. There were calls to suspend or even deregister the champion. In the end there was an apology and a $20 000 fine. The AFL made their point very clearly — no criticism of the umpires was going to be tolerated. Many felt Hird's punishment excessive for the crime. Then again Dick Condon might have thought Hird got off lightly.

The King

Wagga Wagga is an epicentre of sporting talent. The town has produced Mark Taylor (former Australian Cricket captain), Paul Kelly (former captain of the Sydney Swans), Laurie Daley (former Rugby League Captain) and Wayne Carey (the King, and former captain of the Kangaroos).

The King dominated football in the 1990s like no other player. He was strong, athletic, skilled and arrogant. His unique strut gave him a second nickname, Duck. Kangaroo fans loved him as much as the opposition fans hated him. In one newspaper's poll, he was consistently voted as the most hated footballer in the competition, but no doubt those same people who voted for him would have had him playing for their team in a blink of an eye. Like Leigh Matthews before him, Carey was an inspirational leader and the Kangaroos were envied by the rest of the competition for the close relationships developed within the team.

The cash-strapped Roos relied on Carey for his football brain and his marketing potential. He captained the Roos to three grand finals for two flags. He was All Australian—the experts' theoretical best team for the year—seven times and voted by his peers as the most valuable player twice.

But as sensational as he was on the field, off it, he was not perfect. In 2002 every Shinboner's heart was ripped out when Carey left the Roos after he admitted having an affair with Kelli Stevens, the wife of his vice captain and good mate, Anthony. The media went into hysteria. Front and back pages of the local newspapers were dedicated to the incident. News reporters camped out trying to get an exclusive interview with him or his wife Sally. Carey headed to the United States for a holiday to escape the attention. How much had football changed? This was hardly the first time something like this had happened in a football club, but in the past there was a silent agreement that these things were personal and not to be reported. It raised an interesting question — what is newsworthy?

> *"King's reign ends in tears, disgrace"*
>
> *"I'm sorry: Carey quits over affair with teammate's wife"*
>
> *"Captain Kangaroo bounces back Cowboy Carey"*
>
> *"Shattered Carey finds refuge with family"*
>
> *"The King puts his old courtiers to the sword"*
>
> *"Do we really want this adulterer in our team?"*
>
> *"Star 'in a bedroom, crying his heart out'"*
>
> *"Carey the victim throws Kelli Stevens to wolves"*
>
> *"EXCLUSIVE: CAREY TELLS MY SHAME 'I love Sally…this is the biggest mistake I've ever made'"*
>
> *"Pledge not to sledge over Carey affair"*
>
> *"Duck season"*
>
> Just some of the headlines that appeared in newspapers after the 'Carey affair'.

Anthony Stevens was made captain of the Roos and the team showed that famous Shinboner spirit, doing much better than most experts had predicted, in 2002. After sitting out a year, Carey returned to play for the Adelaide Crows. His first match back against his old club was full of spite. Fascinated fans watched as Stevens repeatedly careered into a defiant Carey. When Steven's great mate and League tough nut, Glen Archer, feinted to punch Carey on the chin, the King flinched and the crowd drew breath. No punch was actually thrown but it had more drama than an all-in brawl.

Women in the ranks

There are women in every aspect of football, except on the field. Australian football boasts one of the highest percentages of female supporters of any football code in the world. Women are strongly represented in the media, behind the scenes as trainers, physios and nutritionists and they sit on many club boards. The clubs rely on the legion of women who volunteer their time. Jill Lindsay has been a senior manager at the AFL for many years. In time we may see a female president of a club. But as prevalent as women are in football the road is often rocky.

In 1996 the first woman, Elaine Canty, was appointed to the tribunal to adjudicate over the reports from the weekend's games. Elaine is a lawyer who also covered sport on the radio. Ron Barassi was one of many who thought Elaine couldn't do the job because she had obviously never played league football. It was pointed out to an embarrassed Ron that four other members of the tribunal had also never played league football. No one had ever questioned their appointment because they were men.

While few will ever play the game as adults, heaps of young girls fantasise about pulling down a screamer or slotting through the winning goal. Now they can join Auskick and have a run on the MCG, Football Park or the SCG at half-time just like the boys. The development of a competition for girls aged between 12 and 17 may see more keep playing on.

It is 20 years since Corrie Perkin covered her first game. Scan the sports pages of any of the major newspapers today and you will be struck not by the lack of female footy reporters, but the abundance of them. Women too, are well represented as boundary riders — reporting the game from inside the fence line. In fact it is only as commentators — calling the game for TV viewers or radio listeners — that women are still to make their mark.

Football owes a lot to women — their passion for the game has helped it survive and prosper. Sometimes football has not always respected women. Recently questions have been asked about the 'blokey' nature of footy clubs and the need to change some attitudes towards women within them.

St Kilda were looking the goods in 2004. After so many years in the doldrums its playing list was now one of the best in the competition, and they had just won the

pre-season premiership. Then accusations of rape against two of their players were made public. No charges were laid. Over the next few months more accusations against current players and past were made public, and the topic of sexual assault by footballers was hotly debated in the press. The AFL and the clubs continue to struggle with their responsibility to the players and the women in these situations and what they can do to prevent it happening again. It is an issue they have barely begun to tackle.

Future footy

What will happen to footy in the future? Will there be video umpiring? Three pointers? Nine pointers? How many teams will be playing and where will they come from? Will footy survive? Sometimes to see into the future we first need to look back.

What has changed since Tom Wills was pulling down marks and kicking goals? The grounds are bigger, grander and the turf lusher, but the MCG is still the home of football. The footballers are bigger, faster and command generous salary packages. Tom might be a little disturbed by the hugging and bum-slapping that goes on after every goal is kicked, but no doubt he would still be impressed by their skill, dedication and courage. In the boardrooms the administrators and club officials are still scrapping, but that would be nothing new to Tom. Would his heart be gladdened to see his two old teams, Melbourne and Geelong, still going strong?

The only thing about the 2005 all non-Victorian AFL grand final that would have surprised Tom, was that it took so long to happen. No doubt he would be a little sad the greatest game in the world is still enjoyed by a relatively small band of lucky fans.

On the ground there are centre circles, centre squares, goal squares, 50-metre lines, point posts and an explosion in the number of umpires. None of this would have worried Tom; the game he played was always fluid.

But what would he make of the bunch of suits that descend on the huddle with whiteboards at quarter-time? When Tom died in 1880, the captain still coached the team and it would be over 20 years before Jack Worrall would become footy's first dedicated coach. Now we have head coach, assistant coaches and specialist coaches. Many fans would trade a champion player for the likes of Matthews, Malthouse, Sheedy or Pagan. The evolution of the coach into business manager, media star and innovator has perhaps been one of football's biggest changes.

Around the country the kids roll up in droves to Auskick but the future of country football, where struggling clubs are merging just to stay afloat, remains a concern.

But perhaps the barracker has been the most enduring sight in football. They're as mad about football now as they were back in Tom's day. They still deck themselves out in their club colours, cheering on their own and jeering the opposition. The cheersquads work hard each week to create their monstrous banners, crepe paper artworks, to inspire the team. Around the ground you can still see perfectly sane men, women and children rugged up in the rain and wind, with a thermos and a hot pie, hanging out for that one miraculous speckie or bone-crunching tackle. We can watch four, five or six games a week on TV, but the ardent fan still wants to be where the action is, hopelessly addicted to that glorious feeling you only get when your team wins a tight one and you were right there with them. And, as long as the fans still come to watch, we will always have a game of our own.

Ted Whitten leaves the MCG supported by his son, Ted Jnr, after taking a lap of honour (Fairfax photos/Michael Rayner).

Footy Speak

Aerial Ping-Pong Insulting name Rugby fans give to Australian Rules.

Ball! Holding the ball while being tackled is against the rules. Amazingly the fans have to constantly remind the umpires of this rule during the game by screaming out "ball!"

Banana Kick Also known as the checkside or backscrew punt. The ball curves after the kick. Used for shots on goal from impossible angles.

Barracker, Fan, Supporter, The Faithful All names for people who love to cheer their team on. A real fan stays true whether their team is favourites for the premiership or heading towards the wooden spoon.

Big Sticks Goalposts. Interestingly no one ever calls the point posts the little sticks.

Big V Victorian state team/jumper.

Bag Several meanings. To kick a bag is to kick a lot of goals in a game—anything over four would qualify. To bag it is to kick a goal, as in 'he bagged it'. To give someone a bagging is to ridicule a player's ability by saying something like, "My mum kicks better than you."

Banner In homage to their heroes, official club cheersquads make huge banners from crepe paper and sticky tape. The banner displays the cheersquad poetry which is meant to inspire the players, who run through it on their way onto the ground. Banner-making is an art—too much sticky tape and the players bounce off or are cut to ribbons on their way through. Despite the poetry being overtaken by corporate sponsorship logos the banner remains one of the iconic Aussie Rules images.
"If you lose to Collingwood in a Grand Final you're a bloody idiot." Carlton banner after Essendon had lost the 1990 Grand Final. Essendon were sponsored by TAC whose slogan was "If you drink and drive,

you're a bloody idiot."
"If Ablett is God, then Malthouse must be his father." West Coast banner in 1992 Grand Final.

BOG Best on Ground. Best player, either side, in a particular game. Everyone has an opinion on just who is BOG, the commentators, the journalists, the umpires and every fan — they rarely agree.

Bomb A long bomb (there is no such thing as a short bomb) is a long kick, usually a torpedo. To bomb it is to kick it.

Brains Trust Unnamed group of individuals who make all the important decisions at a football club.

Cheersquad The most ferociously loyal and one-eyed supporters of all. They make the banners and sit behind the goals during the game, flogging their floggers and dodging the ball.

Cherry, Pill, Pigskin, Sherrin, Leather, Tan Ball The football.

Chewy on ya boot The most famous of Aussie Rules

	taunts, meant to be off-putting to a player kicking for goal.
Clangers	An embarrassing blue made by a player, like kicking the ball straight to the opposition. One of the tallies kept by the statisticians.
Collywobbles	Between 1958 and 1990 Collingwood had a reputation of failing in the grand final. It became known as the Collywobbles.
Croweaters	South Australians.
Crumbers	Players who hang around the outside of the pack waiting for the ball to come free.
Daisy Cutter	A kick where the ball travels very close to the ground.
Floater	A kick where the ball floats in the air. Very hard to judge.
Floggers	Crepe-paper streamers attached to a pole. Shaken by cheersquads to support their team, and to put off the opposition when they are having a shot at goal.
The G	The nickname for the Melbourne Cricket Ground.
Guernsey	Football jumper.

Hard ball Getting the ball in a highly contested pack. Statisticians now keep a tally of how many 'hard ball gets' a player has for the game.

Hi Diddle Diddle Rhyming slang for middle. The shortest path to the goals is straight down the hi diddle diddle.

High Mark, Screamer, Speckie Marking the ball while leaving an impression of your boot-stops on your opponents back. Some would say there is nothing more spectacular in Aussie Rules than watching the big men fly.

Hip and shoulder Pushing another player off the ball using your body. When applying a hip and shoulder you need to keep your elbows in or you might find the umpie writing your name down in the book.

Leather poisoning Might not sound like it, but a good thing to get. A player who gets the ball a lot is said to have leather poisoning.

Man up The second most common cry from supporters, after "Ball!" In the old days players had set positions and

	set opponents, the players manned up on an opponent. These days the game is much more open and many players don't have set positions, but there is nothing more distressing to the fans than to see the opposition roaming loose.
Melee	Those toffs at the AFL have decreed that when the teams fight it's not called a brawl, it's called a melee. Perhaps they think it sounds nicer.
Mongrel punt	A poor kick.
One-eyed	Fans who are so biased they can't even see the other team on the field.
Place kick	Old-style kick. The player makes a mound on the ground, puts the ball there before kicking it. Still used in rugby.
Sausage roll	Rhyming slang for goal.
Shellacking	When your team gets beaten by a lot, they have had a shellacking.
Shepherd	Protecting a team-mate with the ball by running between him and an opponent.
Shirtfront	A head-on charge aimed at knocking over your opponent.

Ton	Hundred goals in a season.
Torpedo	A style of kick that gets plenty of distance.
Two fingers	When the pill goes through the big sticks the umpire signals it's a goal by holding up two fingers.
White maggot	Old expression for umpires because they wore white. Now they wear yellow and orange as well as white, and 'orange maggot' doesn't quite sound right. The umpire is also called the umpie, the man in white and other things I can't repeat. He is never, ever, called the referee.
Wooden Spoon	If at the end of the season you are bottom of the ladder, you have won the wooden spoon. Not something to aspire to. The team that wins the wooden spoon might also be referred to as a cellar dweller.

Acknowledgments

Two books were particularly invaluable in my research of the history of Australian football. Geoffrey Blainey's *A Game of Our Own: the Origins of Australian Football* gives a vibrant account of the early years of Australian football and I have referenced a number of the historian's conclusions in *Shirtfront*. Rob Hess and Bob Stewart's *More than a Game* is a detailed and engaging report of football from the first game to the dawning of the new millennium.

Special thanks goes to historian David Allen and Alison Arnold, Andrew Kelly and Maryann Ballantyne at black dog books. David's unmatchable knowledge of Australian football, attention to detail and encouragement has been invaluable. David has forgotten more about Australian football than most of us ever knew. Without Ali and the rest of the black dog crew this book would not have been written; thanks guys.

The official AFL website, www.afl.com.au, is a valuable resource and provides links to all the AFL club sites and the various state organising bodies. The website for the International Australian Football Council, www.iafc.com.au also provided interesting information about football outside the realm of the AFL.

I have also drawn from other publications for some of the more fabulous stories that make Australian football the game we love. The key sources follow:

Atkinson, Graeme and Hanlon, Michael, *3AW Book of Footy Records*, Matchbooks, 1989.

Barassi, Ron and McFarline, Peter, *Barassi: the life behind the legend*, Simon & Schuster Australia, 1995.

Blainey, Geoffrey, *A Game of Our Own: the Origins of Australian Football*, Black Inc., 2003.

Flanagan, Martin, *1970 & Other Stories of the Australian Game*, Allen & Unwin, 1999.

Flanagan, Martin, *The Game in Time of War,* Pan Macmillian, 2003.

Hansen, Brian, *The Blue Boys, the history of the Carlton Football Club from 1864*, Brian Hansen Nominees, 2002.

Hess and Stewart (eds), *More than a game: an unauthorised history of Australian rules football*, Melbourne University Press, 1998.

Holt, S. and Hutchinson, G. (eds), *Footy's Greatest Players*, Coulomb Communications, 2003.

Main, Jim and Allen, David, *Fallen—The Ultimate Heroes: footballers who never returned from war*, Crown Content, 2002.

Main, Jim, *More than a century of AFL Grand Finals*, Pennon Publishing, 2001.

Mancini, A. and Hibbins, G.M. (eds), *Running with the Ball: Football's Foster Father*, Lynedoch Publications, 1987.

Sheedy, Kevin and Brown, Carolyn, *Football's Women: the Forgotten Heroes*, Penguin Books, 1998.

Tatz, Ramsey, Stocks, Bass, Winkler, Eva, Quayle and Blake, *AFL's Black Stars*, Thomas C. Lothian, 1998.

Black Dog Books would like to thank the Dyer family for their kind permission in allowing Jack Dyer's image to be reproduced on the cover, and Maria and Ross of Carnegie Collectibles (www.carnegiecollectables.com.au) for allowing us to photograph their collection of cigarette cards.

Images

Pages 4–5 Football in Yarra Park, 1874 (LaTrobe Picture Collection, State Library of Victoria).

Pages 32–3 1904 Sniders and Abraham Standard Cork Tipped Cigarette Cards featuring J Smith, T Beecham, C Rowlands, M Donaghy.

Pages 50–1, 59 Enlist in the Sportsmen's Thousand, 1915 (Troedel Collection, La Trobe Picture Collection, State Library of Victoria).

Pages 70–1 Haydn Bunton Snr (Newspix).

Pages 96–7 Ron Barassi (Fairfax photos).

Pages 120–1 Gary Ablett (Newspix/Norm Oorloff).

Pages 146–7 Nicky Winmar (Fairfax photos/Wayne Ludbey).

Pages 166–7 Tony Lockett (Newspix/Phil Hillyard).

Headlines

"King's reign ends in tears, disgrace" *Herald Sun* 14/3/2002

"I'm sorry: Carey quits over affair with teammate's wife" *The Age* 14/3/2002

"Captain Kangaroo bounces back Cowboy Carey" *The Age* 27/3/2002

"Shattered Carey finds refuge with family" *The Age* 15/3/2002

"The King puts his old courtiers to the sword" *Sun Herald* 4/5/2002

"Do we really want this adulterer in our team?" *Sun Herald* 11/8/2002

"Star 'in a bedroom, crying his heart out'" *Sun Herald* 17/3/2002

"Carey the victim throws Kelli Stevens to wolves" *The Age* 7/8/2002

"EXCLUSIVE: CAREY TELLS MY SHAME 'I love Sally...this is the biggest mistake I've ever made'" *Herald Sun* 15/3/2002

"Pledge not to sledge over Carey affair" *Herald Sun* 5/4/2002

"Duck season" *Herald Sun* 12/7/2002

Index

… thank you for reading books from black dog